IRISH HISTORIC HOUSES

Kevin O'Connor

Gill & Macmillan

Published in Ireland
by Gill & Macmillan Ltd
Goldenbridge, Dublin 8
with associated companies throughout the world

Created and produced by
Eric Dobby Publishing Ltd
All enquiries for rights to
12 Warnford Road, Orpington, Kent BR6 6LW, UK

A catalogue record is available for this book from the British Library.

ISBN: 0-7171-2395-2

For

Patricia O'Connor

Castletown House

CONTENTS

Kilkenny Castle

MAP OF IRELAND

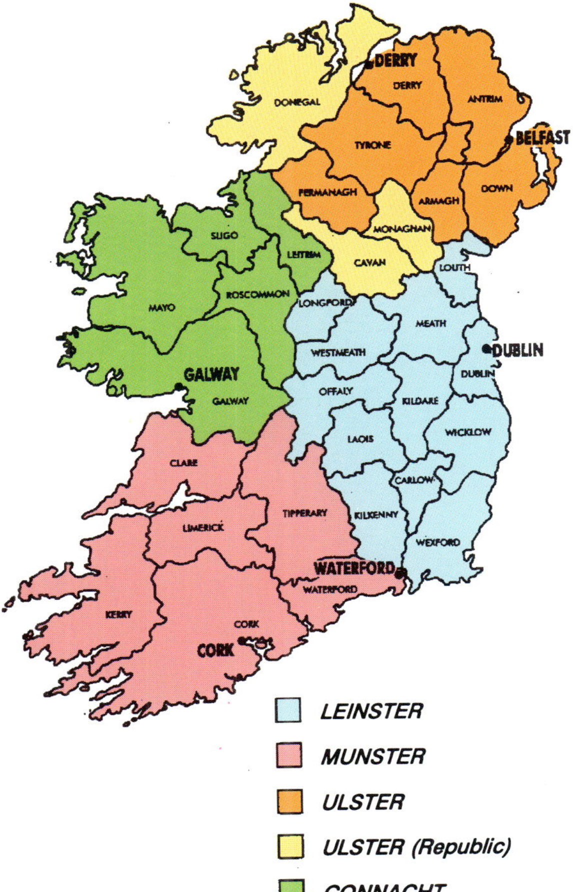

Craggaunowen - The Living Past

INTRODUCTION

The historic houses and homes found throughout Ireland are part of its heritage. They provide a rich variety of places to visit, explore and enjoy, ranging from simple cottages to great palaces full of priceless treasures. Some have changed very little since they were built, and remain occupied by the families who built them; others have changed greatly and would not be recognised today by their founders.

Ireland's architecture reflects her history. A listing of the ruins in Ireland is a testimony to the turbulence of life. Before the 18th century defensive towers with few or no windows, surrounded by a walled enclosure called a *bawn*, provided security as well as a home. This ancient design is thought to have descended directly from the prehistoric Celtic forts. As conditions settled mansions such as Portumna or Ormond Castle in Carrick-on-Suir were built within walls. There was also the emergence of the 'long house', such as Cratloe Woods House, a relatively unsophisticated design.

Then came the remarkable flowering of Palladian palaces and stately homes, as the 'Ascendancy' (mostly of English origin) celebrated their wealth and social and political status. Dublin developed into a Georgian city, one of the most beautiful in Europe, with fine houses displaying the artistic plasterwork of the 'stuccodores', Italian craftsmen who were soon surpassed in skill by their native pupils.

Right into the late 19th century the rich adapted to the changing styles as they built their houses. 'Castles' in neo-Gothic style (such as Tullynally) flaunted more towers and battlements than ever appeared on real castles. However, the religious and political divide meant that while landlords lived sometimes in great splendour, their tenants often held land on very poor terms. The Union with the United Kingdom did not have the benefits hoped for, and the Great Famine in the 1840s dealt the death blow to landlordism. Starving peasants could not pay rents and landlords were forced to move from the mansions they could no longer afford to maintain. Some never returned.

In the second half of the 19th century as the political will and economic power of the landlords crumbled, so too did their houses. Many fine houses that were not ruined by neglect were burnt down in the Troubles of the 1920s. Once there were an estimated 1,000 great houses; now few remain.

Of those that survived some are now hotels, government offices or golf clubs. Bunratty is world-famous for its medieval banquets, while Westport is a huge holiday centre. However, the Irish Georgian Society has rescued many fine buildings and the Irish State has done some remarkable restoration on others, while in Northern Ireland the National Trust has rescued several.

Irish Historic Houses is not just about the 'Big Houses'. It also includes the cottages and small houses of historic or literary interest. The Ulster and Bunratty Folk Parks illustrate vernacular architecture and the Irish literary heritage is represented by the Martello Tower featured in James Joyce's *Ulysses* and Yeats' famous Tower at Thoor Ballylee. There are also buildings associated with the great political figures of Parnell, Castlereagh, Pearse and President Arthur of the United States.

Irish Historic Houses includes the great majority of those houses and homes which are of architectural, artistic and historic interest, and which are open to the public. The listing is arranged in sections, according to the four ancient provinces of Ireland - Leinster, Munster, Ulster and Connacht. The counties of each province are then arranged in alphabetical order and the houses alphabetically (approximately) within each of these counties. Ulster is further divided into Northern Ireland and the Republic as the northern counties of Cavan, Donegal and Monaghan are part of the Republic. Full colour illustrations accompany each entry, as well as all the available information needed when planning a visit. There is a concise description of each house - its history, inhabitants, contents and architecture - followed by details of any grounds, parks, gardens or surroundings. Directions are also given, along with details of opening dates and hours, admission charges, parking and picnic areas, places to eat and shops. Access for visitors in wheelchairs is also noted. Although every effort has been made to verify all the details provided, readers (especially those in large groups or with special needs) are advised to check beforehand, as there may be some changes.

Finally, I would like to thank Anne Grady of the Irish Office of Public Works for all her help as well as the National Trust and the owners and managers of the properties listed here who have proved so helpful in providing information and photographs.

IRISH HISTORIC HOUSES

Castletown House: Staircase and Entrance Hall

LEINSTER HISTORIC HOUSES

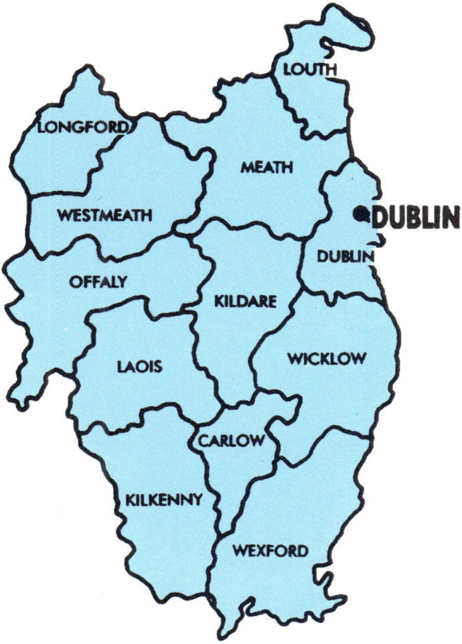

Co. Dublin
Ardgillan Castle
Ashtown Castle
Ayesha Castle
Casino
Dublin Castle
James Joyce Tower
Malahide Castle
Newbridge House
Newman House
Number Twenty Nine
Powerscourt Townhouse
Rathfarnham Castle
Royal Hospital
St. Enda's School (Pearse Museum)

Co. Kildare
Castletown House

Co. Kilkenny
Kilkenny Castle

Co. Laois
Emo Court

Co. Longford
Carriglas Manor

Co. Offaly
Birr Castle
Charleville Forest Castle

Co. Westmeath
Belvedere House
Tullynally Castle

Co. Wexford
Johnstown Castle

Co. Wicklow
Avondale House
Humewood Castle
Kilruddery House
Russborough House

ARDGILLAN CASTLE

Balbriggan, Co. Dublin Tel: 01 8492212
Off N1 Dineehen Lusk/Skerries on R127

Ownership: Fingal County Council

General Description: The central part of this large, castellated country manor was built in 1738 by Robert Taylor with the west and east wings added later in the century. It was the family home of the Taylors until 1962. The drawing-, dining- and morning-rooms and library are furnished in Georgian or Victorian style. The upstairs rooms are used for exhibitions.
Features of the grounds include the Walled Garden, Yew Walk and the haunted Lady's Stairs footbridge.

Open: 1st April to 30th September, daily (except Monday) and Public Holidays, 11.00-6.00; 1st February to 30th March, 1st October to 20th December, 11.00-4.30.

Admission: £2.50; Senior Citizen/Student £1.50; Family £5.00.

Facilities: Tea-rooms within the Castle open as per Castle times. Coffee shop in park (the former Head Steward's house) open from 1st June to 31st August, 1.30-5.30. Car park.

Disabled Access: Yes.

Additional Information: There is a permanent exhibition of maps including the complete 17th-century Down Survey of Ireland.

Special Events: The Castle regularly hosts art exhibitions as well as the North Dublin Craft Workers Exhibition in June.

Ardgillan Castle

ASHTOWN CASTLE

Phoenix Park, Dublin Tel: 01 6770095
4km from the centre of Dublin, next to the Phoenix Park Visitor Centre

Ownership: Irish State

General Description: A typical defensive tower house, which probably dates from the 17th century, located in the heart of Phoenix Park.

Open: January to mid-March, November and December, Saturday and Sunday, 9.30-4.30; mid to end March, October, daily, 9.30-5.00; June to September, daily, 9.30-6.30.

Admission: £2.00; Senior Citizen £1.50; Child/Student £1.00; Family £5.00.

Facilities: Coffee shop and restaurant. Visitor Centre presenting the history of Ireland from 3500 BC to the present. Film show (24 mins). Nature Trails. Toilets. Car park.

Disabled Access: To ground floor only. Toilet.

AYESHA CASTLE

Victoria Road, Killiney, Co. Dublin Tel: 01 2852323
12km from Dublin

Ownership: Mrs Bridget Aylmer

General Description: A romantic 19th-century Victorian castle with the finest views of Killiney Bay and Sugarloaf Mountain in the county. It was built from local granite by Robert Warren, a wealthy landowner in 1840, when he called it Victoria Castle. It was gutted by fire in 1926 and was bought and renovated by Sir Thomas Power of Power's Whiskey who renamed it Ayesha, after the goddess heroine of Rider Haggard's novel *She*, who rose, phoenix-like, from the flames. Amongst its notable features are the fine oak panelling in the entrance hall and dining-room, and the magnificent spiral staircase.

Open: March 1st to 31st, 10.00-2.00; April/May, Tuesday to Friday, 2.00-6.00; June/July, Saturday to Monday, 11.00-3.00.

Admission: £2.50 (main house and garden); £3.00 (main house, garden and arts and crafts gallery); Senior Citizen/Child £1.75.

Facilities: Restaurant serving lunches and teas (guided tour and afternoon tea £5.00). Car park and toilets.

Disabled Access: None.

Additional Information: Victorian evenings (meal and entertainment £35); poetry reading evenings with supper (£15).

Special Events: Regular exhibitions of family lace and local history. Series of exhibitions by internationally famous Irish artists.

CASINO, MARINO

Marino, Dublin 3 Tel: 01 8331618
5 miles from Dublin city centre, off the Malahide Road, Dublin 3

Ownership: Irish State

General Description: One of the loveliest 18th-century classical buildings in Ireland, perfect in every detail. The so-called Casino (it has nothing to do with gambling) was designed as a garden pleasure house for the Earl of Charlemont by Sir William Chambers in 1769. The actual construction in Lord Charlemont's garden was by Simon Vierpyl, and cost an incredible £60,000. It is covered in the most delicately executed decorations in the Classical style and, although it looks tiny, it has in fact eight rooms, a staircase and a basement.

Open: November, February to mid-June, Sunday and Wednesday, 12.00-4.00; mid-June to September, daily, 9.30-6.30; October, daily, 10.00-5.00.

Admission: £2.00; Senior Citizen £1.50; Child/Student £1.00; Family £5.00.

Facilities: Car park. Toilets.

Disabled Access: No, since interior is accessed by a stair.

Additional Information: Visits with a guided tour only. No dogs.

DUBLIN CASTLE

Dame Street, Dublin 2 Tel: 01 6797831

Ownership: Irish State

General Description: The Castle is the heart of historic Dublin, built on the Black Pool - Dubh Linn - from which the city gets its name. Formerly housing the vice-regal administration and residence, it was fort, prison, treasury and courts before being handed over to the new state of Ireland. It is now the venue for Ireland's Presidencies of the EU, Presidential inaugurations and State functions. The gilded splendour of the magnificent State Apartments, built as the residential quarters for the vice-regal court, makes them well worth a visit. Visitors may also see the Chapel Royal and the medieval Undercroft, where part of the original Viking fortress is on view.

Open: Guided tours only Monday to Friday, 10.00-5.00; Saturday, Sunday and Public Holidays, 2.00-5.00.

Admission: £2.00; Child/Student/OAP £1.00.

Facilities: Restaurant and craft shop. No car park.

Disabled Access: None.

Additional Information: The State Apartments are occasionally closed at short notice for EU meetings.

JAMES JOYCE TOWER

Joyce Tower, Sandycove, Co. Dublin Tel: 01 2809265
1 mile south-east of Dun Laoghaire on the coast road to Sandycove.
Bus No 8 or DART.

Ownership: Dublin Tourism.

General Description: Built by the British Army as a fortress, it was James Joyce's celebrated novel *Ulysses* which firmly established the fame of this Martello Tower as a most unlikely home. The opening chapter features 'stately, plump Buck Mulligan' coming from the stairhead and then describes the Round Room where the three men have breakfast. This room has been reconstructed exactly as described in the novel. Joyce stayed there (briefly) as a guest of Oliver St John Gogarty in September 1904. The Tower also features a museum of Joyce memorabilia.

Open: April to October, Monday to Saturday, 10.00-5.00 (closed 1.00-2.00); Sunday and Public Holidays 2.00-6.00; November to March by appointment.

Admission: £2.20; Concessions (OAP, under-18, unwaged) £1.80; Child (3-11) £1.10; Family £6.50.

Facilities: Bookshop. Street parking only.

Disabled Access: Limited to ground floor only.

Additional Information: No dogs. Street parking only.

Special Events: Annual Bloomsday celebrations 16th June (Tower open 8.00-6.00).

NEWMAN HOUSE

85-86 St Stephen's Green, Dublin 2 Tel: 01 7067122

Ownership: University College Dublin

General Description: These two superb Georgian townhouses boast some of Ireland's finest 18th-century plasterwork. They also have great literary significance from their association with John Henry Newman, the poet Gerard Manley Hopkins (who taught here) and the writers James Joyce and Flann O'Brien (who were students). Number 85, built in 1738 for the MP Hugh Montgomery by Richard Cassell, was among the first of its type in Dublin. Number 86 was finished in 1765. Together they display the development of Irish stucco plasterwork, from the later baroque style to fully-fledged Irish rococo. After passing through other private hands the houses were purchased by the Catholic University of Ireland in the late 19th century. Gerard Manley Hopkins died here whilst Professor of Classics. His study in No 86 is open to the public. Special features include the Apollo Room, a small reception room, whose walls are covered with a rich assembly of plasterwork by the Swiss Francini brothers. The Saloon is one of Ireland's most spectacular interiors.
University College Dublin began the work of restoration in 1989 which has restored much of these two houses to their original splendour.

Open: June to August, Tuesday to Friday, 10.00-4.30; Saturday 2.00-4.30; Sunday 11.00-2.00. Other times by appointment.

Admission: £2.00; Senior Citizen/Student £1.00.

Facilities: No facilities available.

Disabled Access: None.

MALAHIDE CASTLE

Malahide, Co. Dublin Tel: 01 8462184
8 miles north of Dublin. No 42 bus and suburban rail.

Ownership: Fingal County Council

General Description: The oldest part of this ancient family home is the keep-like tower which dates from the 14th century. When the last Lord Talbot died in 1973 his family had lived here for 791 years. Standing in 250 acres of park in a built-up area, the castle looks splendidly military; but inside it reflects immense luxury. The Great Hall is the oldest medieval hall in Ireland. The Oak Room is dominated by superb 16th-century Flemish carved wood panels. The 18th century is represented by the library, with its gilt and hand-painted leather wall hangings. The elaborate, almost rococo, drawing-rooms were constructed between 1765 and 1783 and have plaster ceilings by Robert West.
Among the furniture in these rooms are a pair of gilt settees in the French style of about 1770, an excellent Bossi table and a gilt mirror by John and Francis Booker of about 1765.
The Castle also houses a large collection of paintings from the National Portrait Collection of the National Gallery of Ireland.
Visitors can walk through the grounds with their woods, parkland and exotic shrubs. They were created by Milo, Lord Talbot de Malahide between 1948 and 1973.

Open: January to December, Monday to Friday, 10.00-5.00; November to March, Saturday, Sunday and Public Holidays, 2.00-5.00. April to October, Saturday, 11.00-6.00, Sunday and Public Holidays, 11.30-6.00.

Admission: £2.85; Concessions and under-18 £2.30; Child (3-11) £1.50.

Facilities: Cafe, restaurant and craft shop. Car park. Toilets.

Disabled Access: None.

Additional Information: Picnicking facilities. No dogs allowed. Banqueting facilities are available within the house.

NEWBRIDGE HOUSE

Donabate, Co. Dublin Tel: 01 8436534
12 miles north of Dublin. Bus No 33B and suburban rail.

Ownership: Fingal County Council

General Description: This solid Georgian mansion was designed by George Semple and built in 1737 for Charles Cobbe, Archbishop of Dublin. The Cobbe family continued to live here until 1985. The red drawing-room, with its crimson walls and floor (c. 1760), is one of the finest Georgian interiors in Ireland with plasterwork of the highest standard attributed to Richard Williams of Dublin, a pupil of Robert West. It was built by the Archbishop's fashionable daughter-in-law to show off her husband's collection of fine paintings. The dining-room features a lovely rococo ceiling and a magnificent pier mirror made by Cranfield of Dublin, as well as a pair of unusual Chippendale side tables. The kitchen, still largely as it was in the 18th century, has many fascinating fittings and utensils. The Museum of Curiosities is an unusual feature of the house. It is one of very few family museums to survive and displays weird and wonderful objects collected around the world over two centuries by the family. To the rear of the house is a late 18th-century cobbled courtyard. The visitor can visit the dairy, carpenter's shop, forge, stables and labourers' cottages and see their original tools, implements and furniture as well as the traditional working farm where he/she can follow the annual life cycle of the farm animals.

The demesne of 370 acres consists of pastureland, woods, watercourses and pleasure grounds.

)pen: April to September, Tuesday to Friday, 10.00-5.00, Saturday 1.00-6.00, Sunday and Public Holidays, 2.00-6.00; October to ɅIarch, Saturday, Sunday and Public Holidays, 2.00-5.00.

\dmission: £2.60; Concessions and under-18 £2.30; Child (3-11) :1.45.

'acilities: Cafe. Craft shop. Picnicking facilities and car park.

)isabled Access: None.

\dditional Information: Traditional working farm with rare ›reeds of pigs, cattle, sheep, ponies and hens on display. No dogs.

The Dining-room

NUMBER TWENTY NINE

29 Lower Fitzwilliam Street, Dublin 2 Tel: 01 7026165
Corner of Lr Fitzwilliam St/Upr Mount St

Ownership: Electricity Supply Board and National Museum of Ireland

General Description: Number 29 is a completely-restored middle-class house of the late 18th century. It was built in 1794 by John Usher for Mrs Olivia Beatty. From the basement to the attic the house displays a unique collection of furniture, artefacts, works of art and meticulous reconstructions from the house's heyday. Every detail has been lovingly restored and there is something for everyone, from the fully-fitted 18th-century kitchen to the amazing large-scale playhouses and doll's-houses of the 1820s.

Open: Tuesday to Saturday, 10.00-5.00; Sunday 2.00-5.00 (closed two weeks prior to Christmas).

Admission: £2.50; Student, unwaged, elderly £1.00; Under-16 free.

Facilities: Tea-room for snacks. Gift shop.

Disabled Access: None.

Additional Information: Parking only on street meters. No dogs. Guided tours only.

Special Events: Music in the drawing-room in the evening April and October. Evening talks in the atrium.

Number Twenty Nine, Lower Fitzwilliam Street

POWERSCOURT TOWNHOUSE

59 South William Street, Dublin 2 Tel: 01 6794144
Just off Grafton Street

General Description: When the 4th Viscount Powerscourt, Richard Wingfield, built his palatial and fashionable townhouse in 1774 he could not have imagined what would happen to it in the 20th century. The palazzo was originally laid out around an open square. This has now been filled (and covered) in to provide a centre specialising as a grand emporium for crafts, antiques, shopping and restaurants.
Robert Mack built the original house of cut stone between 1771 and 1774. Today you can visit the hall and salon to see the magnificent rococo plasterwork of James McCullough and Michael Reynolds and the fine mahogany staircase.

Open: Monday to Saturday, 9.00-6.00; late night Thursday to 7.00.

Admission: Not applicable.

Facilities: Restaurants and shops.

Disabled Access: Yes.

Additional Information: No dogs allowed.

Special Events: There are frequent special events free of charge including lunchtime recitals, jazz concerts, flower demonstrations, fashion shows and art exhibitions.

RATHFARNHAM CASTLE

Rathfarnham, Dublin 14 Tel: 01 4939462
Off Rathfarnham Avenue, near Bushy Park

Ownership: Irish State

General Description: The date of the foundation of the Castle is uncertain; but recent research suggests 1593 as the likely date when one Adam Loftus, a Yorkshireman, Archbishop of Dublin and Lord Chancellor of Ireland, built it. It is the only 16th-century building to survive in Dublin but features from other periods include some wonderful 18th-century plasterwork. It has a colourful history, most notably in 1649 when it was the Confederate base for their attack on Dublin.
Conservation work is ongoing on site. Access by guided tour only.

Open: Easter, Saturday to Monday, 10.00-5.00; June to September, daily, 10.00-6.00; October, daily, 10.00-5.00.

Admission: £1.50; Senior Citizen £1.00; Child/Student 60p; Family £4.00.

Facilities: Tea-room offering hot and cold lunches open all year. Toilets.

Disabled Access: To tea-room only. Toilet.

ROYAL HOSPITAL

Kilmainham, Dublin Tel: 01 6718666
2km from city centre close to Heuston Station

Ownership: Irish State

General Description: This was never a hospital in the modern sense, which is why it merits an entry in this book. A home for old soldiers (pensioners), it was based on Les Invalides in Paris. It was founded by the Duke of Ormond and finished in 1684 (before the similar 'Hospital' at Chelsea) and was the first of those buildings which were to transform Dublin into a city of European standing. The architect was William Robinson, State Surveyor General. Today it is the oldest fully classical building in Ireland and the largest to survive from the 17th century. The buildings ranged around the quadrangle include the Master's Quarters and the Great Hall with its splendid portraits of monarchs and Lord Justices of Ireland. The Vaulted Cellar contains the 19th-century kitchen. The Chapel is adorned with the most spectacular baroque ceiling, a composition of vegetable and floral extravagances. Plans for opening more buildings on the site are in hand. Today the Hospital itself houses the Irish Museum of Modern Art, but it is well worth a visit for its architectural beauties alone. Further buildings on the site will be opened in due course, including the Deputy Master's House, the Adjutant General's House, the 18th-century garden and the former stable buildings.

Open: Tuesday to Saturday, 10.00-5.30; Sunday and Bank Holidays, 12.00-5.30; closed 24th to 26th December.

Admission: Free.

Facilities: Coffee shop. Bookshop. Car park.

Disabled Access: Yes.

Additional Information: Full programme of exhibitions and classical music recitals. Please ring for full details.

ST ENDA'S SCHOOL (PEARSE MUSEUM)

Grange Road, Rathfarnham, Dublin 16 Tel: 01 4934208
Bus No 16 from city centre. Car park off Grange Road.

Ownership: Irish State

General Description: Patrick Pearse, Irish poet, schoolmaster and Nationalist hero, ran a school here before his involvement in the Easter Rising of 1916 led to his death before an English firing squad. The school building itself is now a museum set in lovely grounds and also features Pearse's quarters as they were when he lived here.
There is a 20-minute audio-visual show, *This Man Kept a School.*

Open: November to January, daily, 10.00-1.00, 2.00-4.00; February, March, April, daily, 10.00-1.00; September to October, daily, 2.00-5.00; May to August, daily, 10.00-1.00, 2.00-5.30.

Admission: Free of charge.

Facilities: Tea-rooms open all year. Car park. Toilets.

Disabled Access: Ground floor and Nature Study Centre.

Additional Information: Nature Study Centre, self-guiding trail.

Special Events: Outdoor concerts during summer season.

CASTLETOWN HOUSE

Celbridge, Co. Kildare Tel: 01 6288252
67/67A bus from city centre/By car take Celbridge turn off N4, gates at end of main street

Ownership: Irish State

General Description: Ireland's first, largest and finest Palladian country house was built around 1722 for Speaker William Conolly of the Irish House of Commons - the wealthiest man in Ireland. It houses a fine collection of 18th-century Irish furniture and paintings.

This splendid, elegant house has a large central block linked on each side by graceful colonnaded curtain walls, leading out to the pavilions on the wings. It was initially designed by the Italian architect Alessandro Galilei and completed and built by Edward Lovett Pearce. He also designed the Parliament House (now the Bank of Ireland).

Castletown was not finished, however, until Lady Louisa Lennox restarted work on it in 1758. She was also responsible for creating the Print Room and for the Pompeian-style decorations of the Long Gallery, as well as for commissioning the great staircase by Vierpyl. The House's wonderful stucco is the work of the Francini brothers. There are also many paintings and much period furniture.

The grounds include a two-mile vista to the Conolly Folly or Obelisk in memory of Speaker Conolly. Close to the River Liffey in the front of the house is the Tuscan Temple.

Castletown was bought in the late 1960s by the Hon. Desmond Guinness, founder of the Irish Georgian Society, to save it from property redevelopment. He devoted enormous energy and resources to maintaining the House and restoring its principal rooms to their original splendour. It was transferred to State ownership in 1994.

Open: April to September, Monday to Friday, 10.00-6.00, Saturday 11.00-6.00, Sunday and Public Holidays, 2.00-6.00.

Admission: £2.50; Senior Citizen £1.75; Child/Student £1.00; Family £6.00.

Facilities: Coffee shop in basement.

The Red Drawing-room

The Dining-room

KILKENNY CASTLE

Castlecomer Road, Kilkenny City, Co. Kilkenny Tel: 056 21450
Off the N10 to Knocktopher

Ownership: Irish State

General Description: As the home and principal seat of one of the most powerful of the Norman Irish families, the Butlers, Marquesses and Dukes of Ormond, Kilkenny Castle once dominated the south of Ireland. This 12th-century castle, remodelled in Victorian times, is set in extensive parklands (well worth a visit on their own account). In the 19th century William Robertson undertook a major reconstruction of the castle, in contemporary style, for the 19th Earl of Ormond. Recently restored, the central block displays the library, drawing-room, a bedroom and sitting-room in their full 1830s splendour. The Castle also displays the National Furniture Collection of Ireland. The old Kitchen has been converted to the tea-room. A suite of former servants' rooms has been converted into the Butler Gallery, which mounts frequent exhibitions of contemporary art.

Open: April to May, daily, 10.30-5.00; June to September, daily, 10.00-7.00; October to March, Tuesday to Saturday, 10.30-12.45, 2.00-5.00, Sunday 11.00-12.45, 2.00-5.00.

Admission: £3.00; Senior Citizens £2.00; Child/Student £1.25; Family £7.50.

Facilities: Tea-room. Bookshop. The Butler Gallery. Toilets. Car park. Playground.

Disabled Access: Ground floor and gardens only. Toilet.

Additional Information: Cameras and large bags not allowed on tour. Access by guided tour only.

The Castle Park

The Long Gallery

EMO COURT

Emo, Co. Laois Tel: 0502 26573
Off Portlaoise/Kildare road

Ownership: Irish State

General Description: James Gandon, the architect of Dublin's Custom House, designed Emo Court for John Dawson, Earl of Portarlington, in 1790. The domed rotunda, inspired by the Pantheon in Rome, is one of the most impressive rooms in Ireland. The English architect Lewis Vulliamy added the north front portico with its four giant Ionic columns in 1834.
The formal gardens, amongst the most impressive in Ireland, were first laid out in the 18th century. They feature fine trees, classical statuary and rare shrubs.

Open: Daily, 10.00-6.00.

Admission: £2.00; Senior Citizen £1.50; Child/Student £1.00; Family £5.00.

CHARLEVILLE FOREST CASTLE

Tullamore, Co. Offaly Tel: 0506 21279

Ownership: Vance-Heavey-Alagna family

General Description: Designed in the finest neo-Gothic style around 1798 by Ireland's leading architect of the day, Francis Johnston, a follower of Wyatt, Charleville rises above the trees like some home of the Sleeping Beauty.
This fairytale castle with its towers and turrets was nearly lost through vandalism and neglect while it stood vacant during most of this century. Fortunately, the formal rooms, with their spectacular architectural detail, have survived. After decades lying empty, the Castle is now the home of an Irish-American family who are restoring it to its former glory as their contribution to the heritage of Ireland.

Open: June to September, Wednesday to Sunday and Bank Holidays, 1.00-5.00; September to June and other days, by appointment.

Admission: £3.25; Senior Citizen/Student £2.75; Child £2.00; Family £9.00.

Facilities: Car park. Lunch can be provided if pre-booked.

Disabled Access: None.

Additional Information: Guided tours only. Dogs on leads in grounds only.

CARRIGLAS MANOR

Co. Longford Tel: 043 45165
Take R194 at 2nd roundabout on N4 Longford Bypass to Ballinalee/ Granard (exactly 1 mile to main gate)

Ownership: Mr and Mrs J.G. Lefroy

General Description: The Irish seat of the Huguenot Lefroy family, Carriglas manor was designed by Daniel Robertson and built in 1837 for Thomas Lefroy, Lord Chief Justice of Ireland, a youthful inamorato of Jane Austen. Indeed it is claimed by some of her biographers that she based Darcy, the hero of *Pride and Prejudice*, on the dashing young Thomas Lefroy.
The exterior of the house is Tudor Gothic Revival in style, with gables, oriels and polygonal battlemented turrets in delightful profusion.
Inside, the three main reception rooms interconnect and all have ceilings adorned with plaster ribs and elaborate cornices of flowers and foliage. The drawing-room, which was the main target of a recent burglary, has been refurnished with some fine, recently designed 'Irish' pieces replacing the magnificent collection of early 18th-century continental furniture which was stolen in 1995.
The house is surrounded by 18th-century parkland (with a superb collection of mature trees) and a charming woodland water garden. The grand Georgian stable and farm yards were designed by James Gandon, the renowned architect of other masterpieces such as the Custom House and the Four Courts in Dublin. The buildings extend around two courtyards with pedimented and rusticated archways. They are currently being restored.

Open: House (by appointment only) June to September, Thursday to Monday, 2.00-5.30; Gardens and Costume Museum, 2.00-6.00. Groups welcome any hour by appointment from April to the end of September.

Admission: House tour £1.50; Gardens and Museum, £2.50; Senior Citizen/Student £2.00.

Facilities: Tea-room and gift shop. Car park.

Disabled Access: Yes but not to Museum.

Additional Information: Museum of Victorian Costume. Guided tours only of house. Dogs allowed on lead.

Special Events: Jane Austen Exhibition.

BIRR CASTLE

Co. Offaly Tel: 0506 20056
From Roscrea on N7 (Dublin to Limerick) or Kilbeggan on N4 (Dublin/ Galway road)

Ownership: Private Trust

General Description: In 1620 building commenced on Birr Castle, the family home of the Earl and Countess of Rosse, although much of what we see now is 19th century in origin.
The magnificent gardens and park with their hornbeam allées and tall box hedge - the tallest in the world - were first planted in the 18th century.
The thrilling display of flowering cherries, magnolias and crab apples in spring and the autumn maples and weeping beeches ensure each season is special.

Open: Gardens: January to March and November to December, daily, 9.00-1.00, 2.00-5.00; April to October, daily, 9.00-6.00.

Admission: Gardens: (high season) £3.20, Child £1.60; (low season) £2.60, Child £1.30.

Facilities: Coffee shop known as the 'Castle Kitchen'. Picnic facilities in special scenic spots. Car park.

Disabled Access: Yes to demesne. No to Exhibition Gallery.

Additional Information: The Great Rosse Telescope's restoration is scheduled for completion in October 1996. Dogs on lead only.

Special Events: Chamber concerts in Castle; Georgian Cricket Match (August); Irish Carriage Driving Championships (September).

BELVEDERE HOUSE

Tullamore Road, Mullingar, Co. Westmeath Tel: 044 40861

Ownership: Westmeath County Council

General Description: A fine 18th-century house, notorious for the man who had it built. The 1st Earl of Belvedere discovered that his wife had been unfaithful with one of his brothers and had her locked away for the rest of his life. In the meantime he built this fine house and then found time to quarrel with another brother. So, he built the notorious Jealous Wall, a neo-Gothic folly (an 'Abbey ruin') in the Walled Gardens, to cut off the views across the countryside from Rochfort, his brother's house.

Open: April to October, daily, 12.00-6.00.

Admission: £1.00; Child 50p.

Facilities: Picnic facilities. Car park.

Disabled Access: Yes.

Additional Information: Dogs on lead only.

TULLYNALLY CASTLE

Castlepollard, Co. Westmeath Tel: 044 61159
1.5 miles outside Castlepollard on the Granard road, 13 miles from Mullingar

Ownership: Thomas and Valerie Pakenham

General Description: Stretching for nearly a quarter of a mile, Tullynally Castle is a forest of towers and turrets pierced by a multitude of windows. It has been the seat of the Pakenhams, later Earls of Longford, since 1655 and features as 'Pakenham' in the memoirs of novelist Maria Edgeworth. It is now the largest castle still lived in by a family in Ireland. It is set in lovely parklands and woods next to Lough Derravaragh. The guided tours take in most of the principal rooms, the fine Victorian kitchens and laundries with their amazing gadgets and the magnificent family coach on display in the outer courtyard.
The gardens, covering nearly 30 acres, were laid out in the early 19th century and have been restored recently. They include a walled flower garden, a grotto and two ornamental lakes.

Open: 15th June to 15th August, daily, 2.30-6.00; Gardens: May to September, daily, 2.00-6.00.

Admission: £3.50; Child/Senior Citizen £2.00; Gardens only £2.00; Child/Senior Citizen 50p.

Facilities: Tea-room open weekends and Bank Holidays. Car park.

Disabled Access: Yes.

Additional Information: Picnic sites. Dogs on leads in grounds only.

JOHNSTOWN CASTLE

Research and Development Centre, Co. Wexford Tel: 053 42888
5 miles south west of Wexford town

Ownership: Agricultural and Food Development Authority

General Description: The view of this castellated country house from across the lake is charming. Built in the 19th century in a rather heavy neo-Gothic/Jacobean style, the Castle is a backdrop to the magnificent demesne with its woods, gardens and parkland which spreads out around it. The visitor can wander for hours by its lakes and through the ornamental trees and shrubs.

Open: Grounds: daily, 9.00-5.00.

Admission: Car £2.50; Adults (pedestrian/cyclist) £1.50. Free between 30th September and 26th April.

Facilities: Coffee shop during July and August in Museum. Car park.

Disabled Access: Yes.

Additional Information: Agricultural Museum. Extensive picnic sites. Dogs on lead only.

HUMEWOOD CASTLE

Kilteagan, Co. Wicklow Tel: 0508 73215
Signposted from Baltinglass

Ownership: Private

General Description: Professor Mark Girouard described Humewood as one of the finest and most important 19th-century castellated mansions in Ireland. It was built between 1867 and 1870 for W. Hume Dick MP by the architect William White. A beautiful blend of granite and sandstone, the Castle has remained unaltered since, except for the addition of a ball-room and a circular tower a few years later.
There is a walled estate of almost 200 hectares with two lakes.

Open: 1st May to 15th June, September; visits for groups by appointment at any other time.

Admission: £3.00; Child/OAP £1.50.

Additional Information: The Castle is available for luxury executive accommodation, for corporate or private rental, or conferences. Telephone or fax for details.

KILRUDDERY HOUSE

Bray, Co. Wicklow Tel: 01 2863405
1.5 miles from centre of Bray off Bray/Greystones road

Ownership: Private

General Description: This Elizabethan revival country house was built in 1820 by Richard and William Morrison for the 10th Earl of Meath and incorporates parts of an existing 17th-century house. The drawing-room and dining-room have particularly fine plaster ceilings. In the 1950s the House was reduced in size, but a great deal of the Morrisons' design remains.
The gardens are wonderful examples of baroque landscape. The 4th Earl, Edward, is thought to have laid them out in the late 17th century, which makes them amongst the oldest formal gardens in Ireland. South of the House two canals lead to a round pond and fountain at the end of the vista. Beyond, there is a ha-ha dividing the garden from the park and an avenue of lime trees which leads to a summit over half a mile from the House. East of the House are the Angles - radiating walks flanked by hedges of hornbeam, beech, lime and yew. Westward lies the Wilderness of woods, glades and vistas. Hidden inside you will find a Sylvan Theatre made of a bay hedge, a statue of Venus, a pond and several fountains. In the 17th century even the wilderness had to be under control.

Open: May, June and September, 1.00-5.00 daily. Other times for groups by appointment.

Admission: £2.50; Student and OAP £1.50.

Facilities: Car park. Toilets.

RUSSBOROUGH HOUSE

Blessington, Co. Wicklow Tel: 045 865239
On the N81, 3km S of Blessington

Ownership: Alfred Beit Foundation

General Description: Built in the 18th century and designed by the German Richard Cassell for Joseph Leeson, Earl of Milltown, Russborough House is considered to be Ireland's greatest example of the neo-Palladian style. Begun in 1714, the house took ten years to complete and is constructed of granite. A flight of steps rises up to the front facade, flanked with heraldic lions and urns. Graceful, curved colonnades, crowned on the skyline with baroque urns, sweep out on each side to finely-proportioned wings. Inside there are examples of the plasterwork of the Francini brothers as well as fine furniture, silver, bronzes, porcelain, tapestries and carpets. More importantly it also houses the world-famous Sir Alfred Beit Art Collection. There are two tours, one of the Main Rooms (including paintings) and the other of the Bedrooms (for the porcelain and silver).
The Maze and Rhododendron Garden may be seen by appointment.

Open: April, May, October, Sunday and Bank Holidays, 10.30-5.30; June to August, daily, 10.30-5.30; September, Monday to Saturday, 10.30-2.30, Sunday, 10.30-5.30; also possibly open by prior arrangement at any time.

Admission: Main Rooms: £3.00; Senior Citizen/Student £2.00; Child £1.00; Bedrooms £1.50; Child 50p.

Facilities: Old Kitchen Restaurant. Toilets. Car park.

Disabled Access: Yes.

Additional Information: Picnic site.

Russborough House

AVONDALE HOUSE

Rathdrum, Co. Wicklow Tel: 0404 46111
1 mile from Rathdrum on R752 off N11

Ownership: Coillte Teo (Irish Forestry Board)

General Description: The birthplace and home of Charles Stewart Parnell, the great Parliamentary Nationalist leader, has been refurbished and refurnished to the decor of c. 1850 when he lived here. Samuel Hayes, a barrister and MP in the Irish House of Commons, built the house in 1779 by the banks of the Avonmore River. It passed to the Parnell family in 1795 and on 27th June 1846, Parnell was born there.
Set in 500 acres of forest and parkland, the estate also reflects the work, over nearly a century, of the Irish Forestry Board and their fine plantations can be seen in the walks through the grounds where the wildlife includes badgers, otters, hares and 90 species of bird.

Open: May to September, daily, 10.00-6.00; October to April, 11.00-5.00.

Admission: £2.50; Senior Citizen/Student £1.50; Family £6.00.

Facilities: Coffee shop. Gift shop. Car park.

Disabled Access: Yes, but limited in some areas.

Additional Information: Picnic area. Dogs on leads in grounds only. Audio-visual presentation of life of Parnell (22 mins).

Special Events: Musical evenings in summer. Synge Summer School, Parnell Spring Day, Parnell Summer School.

Avondale House

Avondale House

Avondale House

MUNSTER HISTORIC HOUSES

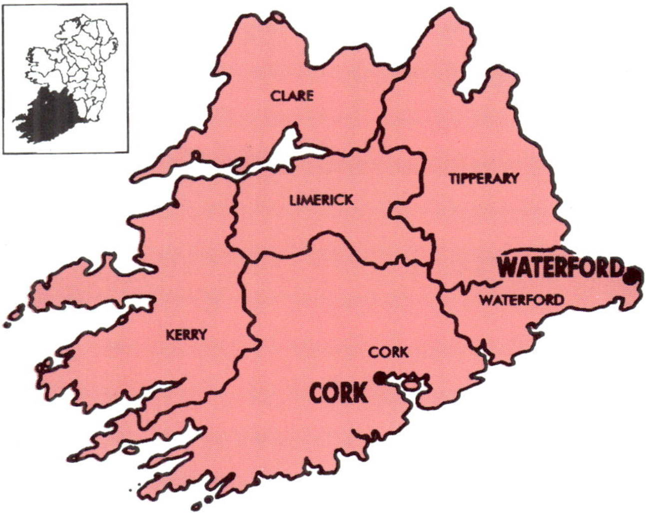

Co. Clare
Bunratty Castle
Bunratty House
Craggaunowen Castle
Cratloe Woods House
Knappogue Castle
Co. Cork
Bantry House
Blarney House
Desmond Castle
Dunkathel House
Riverstown House
Co. Kerry
Derrynane House
Muckross House
Ross Castle
Co. Limerick
Castle Matrix
Glin Castle
Co. Tipperary
Cahir Castle
Damer House
Ormond Castle
The Swiss Cottage
Co. Waterford
Cappoquin House
Curraghmore
Lismore Castle

BUNRATTY HOUSE AND FOLK PARK

Bunratty, Co. Clare Tel: 061 361511
On N18 between Shannon Airport and Limerick

Ownership: Shannon Heritage

General Description: This late Georgian dwelling (built 1805) is of the type built by minor gentry in the 19th century. Between it and the Castle stretches the Folk Park, a collection of buildings moved here from their original sites or reconstructed in authentic style. They range from the one-room dwelling of a landless labourer, through to prosperous farmhouses, as well as the shops and services of the village itself such as the drapers and hardware store and the blacksmith's forge. Most are original buildings transported here from their original site.

Open: Daily, year round, 9.30-5.30.

Admission: Castle and Folk Park £4.75; Child £2.30; Senior Citizen £3.35; Banqueting guest £3.35; Family £11.50. Folk Park only when Castle is closed £3.35; Child £1.85.

Facilities: Tea-room for morning and afternoon teas and snacks. Meals are served in the Barn Kitchen. Mac's Pub serves light lunches.

Disabled Access: Yes.

Additional Information: Picnic sites and full parking. Dogs allowed on leads.

Special Events: You can dine to the accompaniment of a ceili band nightly in the Great Barn.

BUNRATTY CASTLE

Bunratty, Co. Clare Tel: 061 360788
On the main road between Limerick City and Shannon Airport

Ownership: Shannon Heritage

General Description: Bunratty Castle is probably the most complete and authentic medieval castle in Ireland. Built around 1450 by the O'Briens and plundered on many occasions, it was authentically restored in the 1960s to its former medieval splendour with contemporary furnishings and tapestries.
Visitors enter over a drawbridge to the Main Guard. This vaulted room, with its minstrels' gallery, is now used for banquets. The Great Solar has fine oak panelling from c. 1500 and other rooms have superb ceilings of stucco or wood carving. The Castle has some wonderful examples of medieval and early modern furniture and tapestries including a 1661 virginal.

Open: Daily, year round, 9.30-5.30.

Admission: Castle and Folk Park £4.75; Child £2.30; Senior Citizen £3.35; Banqueting guest £3.35; Family £11.50.

Facilities: Tea-room in the Folk Park for morning and afternoon teas and snacks. Mac's Pub in the village serves light lunches.

Disabled Access: Yes.

Additional Information: Picnic sites and full parking. Dogs allowed on leads.

Special Events: Medieval banquets are held nightly in the Castle.

CRAGGAUNOWEN CASTLE

Kilmurry, Sixmilebridge, Co. Clare Tel: 061 367178
Off R469 16km E of Ennis

Ownership: The Hunt Museum Trust

General Description: Craggaunowen Castle is a typical fortified tower of the 15th and 16th centuries - a secure home in troubled times. Built about 1550 by John Mac Sioda Mac Namara, it was later held by the O'Hartigans and Mulchonrys until it was confiscated in Cromwellian times. The Castle was restored by art historian John Hunt who furnished it in the fashion of a 15th or 16th century lord. It houses a selection of his collection of medieval art. But the Castle is not the only ancient dwelling on the site which has been used to bring ancient Celtic times back to life. Exact reproductions of a crannog or lake dwelling made of wattles, reeds and mud can be visited, as well as a furnished 'farmer's house' in a Ring Fort of the 4th or 5th century.
Around the grounds are ancient animal breeds – Soay sheep, Indian Red Jungle fowl, wild boar.

Open: Daily mid-March to end October, 9.00-6.00.

Admission: £3.80; Child £2.50; Senior Citizen/Student £2.75; Family £10.00.

Facilities: Tea, coffee and light meals and teas are served. Visitors' shop. Picnic site. Car park.

Disabled Access: Yes, but not to upper floors of Castle.

Additional Information: There are frequent demonstrations, staff in costume and other features which include a reproduction of St Brendan's boat, an Iron Age wooden road and a hunter's cooking site. Dogs on a lead only.

Special Events: The Celtic festivals of Bealtaine, Lughnasa and Samhain are celebrated at the May, August and October Bank Holidays.

A crannog reconstructed at Craggaunowen

CRATLOE WOODS HOUSE

Cratloe, Co. Clare Tel: 061 327028
Entrance on south side of N18 Limerick-Shannon dual carriageway

Ownership: J. Gordon Brickenden

General Description: Cratloe Woods, part of which dates from the 17th century, is one of the few roofed examples of an Irish 'longhouse' and the only one which is still used as a family home. The longhouse was a uniquely Irish house type which existed from medieval times until the Palladian style overwhelmed the indigenous forms in the 18th century. The house has changed little since Victorian times and features of interest include a pine-panelled dining-room. The house is steeped in history and features works of art, curios and, in the yard, horse-drawn farm machinery and a pets' corner for children. Descendants of the O'Briens, who trace their ancestry to Brian Boru, the 11th-century King of Ireland, still live in Cratloe Woods House.
The estate contains the extensive and ancient Garrannon oak woods which provided beams for Westminster Hall in London and the Royal Palace in Amsterdam. The ruins of Castle Donnell are also in the grounds.

Open: 2nd June to 14th September, daily except Sunday, 2.00-6.00.

Admission: £2.50; Child £1.50; Senior Citizen/Student £1.75.

Facilities: Afternoon teas in the original kitchen in the North Wing. Morning coffee and lunches for groups of 20+ by prior arrangement.

Disabled Access: Most parts can be reached.

Additional Information: Picnic sites. No dogs allowed.

KNAPPOGUE CASTLE

Quin, Co. Clare Tel: 061 360788
2 miles from Quin village on the Ennis-Sixmilebridge road

Ownership: Mark Edwin and Mrs Andrews. Managed by Shannon Heritage.

General Description: Built in 1467 by the McNamara clan, Knappogue Castle was the pride of the forty-two castles they had in the area. It has, over five troubled but colourful centuries of Irish history, succoured friend and foe alike - including Cromwellian troopers who used it in 1641 as a base from which to subdue the neighbourhood. Castellated additions were made in the 19th century by Baron Dunboyne. In recent times it has been restored to its 15th-century style with a fine collection of furniture and boasts some magnificent fireplaces whose blazing fires warm banqueting guests.

Open: April to October, daily, 9.30-5.00.

Admission: £2.55; Child £1.55; Senior Citizen £2.50; Banqueting guest £1.35.

Facilities: Craft shop. Car park.

Additional Information: Medieval banquets with entertainment are held nightly.

BLARNEY HOUSE

Blarney, Co. Cork Tel: 021 385252
5 miles from Cork City

Ownership: Trustees of Blarney Castle Estate

General Description: Although not as well known as its neighbour, Blarney Castle, the House is a fine 19th-century residence. Its military exterior of ashlar, with corner turrets and bartizans with conical roods, makes it look for all the world like one of the grim Scottish Baronial mansions it was based on. The interior is much more domestic, and fabric and furniture have recently been restored. The House stands in splendid formal gardens with a great view of Blarney Castle which is a lovely walk away through the grounds.

Open: June to mid-September, Monday to Saturday, 12.00-6.00.

Admission: House: £2.50; Senior Citizen/Student £2.00; Child over 8 £1.00; **House and Castle:** £5.00; Senior Citizen/Student £3.50; Child £2.00.

Facilities: Two souvenir shops, Bureau de Change, refreshments. Picnic areas and car park.

Disabled Access: Limited.

Additional Information: The Castle, with its world-famous Blarney Stone, is a short walk away along a tree-lined walk. It is open to 6.30 in May and September, to 7.00 in June to August and to 6.00 in October. It is also open on Sundays in summer 9.30 to 5.30, 9.30 to sundown in winter.

Blarney Castle - the House's more famous neighbour

BANTRY HOUSE

Bantry, Co. Cork Tel: 027 50047

Ownership: Shelswell-White family

General Description: The Hutchinson family built their delightful house on the shore of Bantry Bay around 1740. Richard White bought the property in 1765 and added a wing. His son, Richard, the 2nd Earl of Bantry, enlarged it, and filled it with the art treasures he picked up on his European Grand Tour. Among its many rarities are four Aubusson and Gobelin tapestries, said to have been made for Marie Antoinette.
In 1796 a French invasion fleet sailed into Bantry Bay to support a rising planned by the United Irishmen, a revolutionary organisation, but a storm forced them back. The event earned Richard White his peerage for organising local defences.

Open: 17th March to 31st October, daily, 9.00-6.00 (8.00 in summer).

Admission: £4.00; Senior Citizen/Student £2.00.

Facilities: Tea-room. Shop. Museum. Bed and Breakfast and Dinner. Car park.

Disabled Access: Ground floor only.

Additional Information: Picnic sites. Dogs on leads in grounds only.

Special Events: Concerts and other functions.

DESMOND CASTLE

Cork Street, Kinsale, Co. Cork Tel: 021 774855

Ownership: Irish State

General Description: Built as a custom house by the Earl of Desmond around 1500, Desmond Castle has had a colourful history, ranging from Spanish occupation in 1601 to use as a prison for captured American sailors during the American War of Independence. It is known locally as 'The French Prison' after a tragic fire in which 54 prisoners, mainly French seamen, died in 1747. The Castle was also used as a borough jail from 1791 to the onset of the Great Famine when it housed an auxiliary workhouse tending for the starving populace.

Open: Mid-April to mid-June, Tuesday to Sunday and Bank Holidays, 10.00-1.00, 2.00-5.00; mid-June to mid-September, daily, 9.00-6.00; mid-September, Monday to Saturday, 9.00-5.00; early October, Sunday, 10.00-5.00.

Admission: £1.00; Senior Citizen 70p; Child/Student 40p; Family £3.00.

Facilities: None.

Disabled Access: Access is by stone staircase.

Additional Information: Admission charges may increase if the wine museum opens.

DUNKATHEL HOUSE

Glanmire, Co. Cork Tel: 021 821014
N25 3 miles from Cork

Ownership: Russell family

General Description: This fine late 18th-century neo-classical mansion was built c. 1790 on high ground which overlooks the beautiful estuary of the River Lee. The architect, Hargreaves, designed a finely-proportioned interior, with Adam-style chimney-pieces and a particularly elegant bifurcating staircase of Bath stone with an intricate iron balustrade. On the half landing stands the sensuous statue of the Three Graces.
In the hall is a rare late 19th-century orchestrion, built by Imhoff and Muckle, which may be played on request. There is also a collection of Victorian watercolours by Beatrice Gubbins.

Open: May to mid-October, Wednesday to Sunday, 2.00-6.00.

Admission: £2.00; OAP/Student £1.50; Child £1.00.

Facilities: Car park. Teas and luncheons by arrangement.

Disabled Access: Ground floor only.

The Drawing-room

RIVERSTOWN HOUSE

Riverstown, Glanmire, Co. Cork Tel: 021 821205
6km from Cork City on the old Cork to Dublin road

Ownership: Dennis Dooley

General Description: 'the pleasant seat of the lord Bishop of Cork ... a house beautified with several curious pieces of stucco performed by the Francini brothers. The river of Glanmire runs through the gardens banked with serpentine canals ... the grounds of this very respectable seat abound in aged timber and the whole demesne wears an air of dignified seclusion.' Contemporaries thought highly of this house which the bishop rebuilt, with its rather stolid exterior, in 1745. The plasterwork alone is worth a visit, second only to Carton House which is now closed to the public. The house also features period furniture, paintings and sculpture, and a truly magnificent Waterford chandelier of over a thousand pieces of crystal.

Open: May to September, Wednesday to Saturday, 2.00-6.00.

Admission: £2.00.

Facilities: Car park.

Disabled Access: None.

Additional Information: No dogs allowed in house.

DERRYNANE HOUSE

Caherdaniel, Co. Kerry Tel: 066 75113
On the Ring of Kerry road at Caherdaniel village

Ownership: Irish State

General Description: Derrynane House is the ancestral home of Daniel O'Connell, the Liberator, one of the greatest leaders of the Irish people and the statesman who won Catholic emancipation. He himself completed the house in the 1820s. Inside there are family portraits and furniture, as well as the personal belongings and triumphal chariot of the 'Liberator'. There is a collection of silver given to him by grateful Catholics and a remarkable table carved, over four years, by two men. The house is set in a magnificent landscape, 120 hectares (300 acres) of parklands, which include gardens and rare plants, woodlands, sand dunes, Abbey Island, sandy beaches and a nature trail.

Open: 1st March to 30th April and October, Tuesday to Sunday, 1.00-5.00; 1st May to 30th September, Monday to Saturday, 9.00-6.00, Sunday 11.00-7.00; November to February, Saturday and Sunday, 1.00-5.00.

Admission: £2.00; Senior Citizen £1.50; Child/Student £1.00; Family £5.00.

Facilities: Audio-visual show of the life and times of Daniel O'Connell. Cafe. Picnic sites. Car parking.

Disabled Access: Ground floor only. Toilet.

Additional Information: No dogs allowed.

MUCKROSS HOUSE

Killarney National Park, Killarney, Co. Kerry Tel: 064 31440
6km from Killarney on N71 (Kenmare Road)

Ownership: Irish State

General Description: Henry Arthur Herbert built the house, in the best neo-Elizabethan style, in 1843, in the centre of one of the finest landscapes in Ireland. Today it is a centrepiece of the National Park. The house, besides containing beautifully furnished rooms, is a centre of Kerry folk life with exhibitions, craft workshops and a nearby traditional farm.

Open: November to mid-March, daily, 9.00-5.30; mid-March to June, September, October, daily, 9.00-6.00; July and August, daily, 9.00-7.00. **Farm:** 17th March to April, weekends and Bank Holidays, 2.00-6.00; May, October, daily, 2.00-6.00; June to September, daily, 10.00-7.00.

Admission: £3.30; Senior Citizen £2.20; Child/Student £1.50; Family £8.00: **House and Farm** £4.50; Senior Citizen £3.50; Child/Student £2.50; Family £12.00.

Facilities: Restaurant. Craft shop. Car park. Toilets.

Disabled Access: Access to basement and ground floor. Toilet.

Additional Information: 20 min audio-visual show at the Park Visitor Centre. The farm preserves in real life the farming traditions of rural Ireland's past.

ROSS CASTLE

Killarney, Co. Kerry Tel: 064 35851
2km from Killarney, off N71 (Kenmare Road)

Ownership: Irish State

General Description: Ross is a typical Irish chieftain's stronghold from the late Middle Ages. Its foundation date is unsure, but it was probably built in the early 15th century by one of the O'Donoghue Ross chieftains. It is surrounded by a fortified bawn - its curtain walls defended by circular flanking towers, two of which remain. Much of the bawn was removed by the time the Barrack Building was added on the south side of the castle in the latter half of the 17th century. The Castle's interior is furnished with pieces from the 16th and 17th centuries.

Open: April, daily, 11.00-6.00; May, daily, 10.00-6.00; June to September, 9.00-6.00; October, daily, 9.00-5.00.

Admission: £2.50; Senior Citizen £1.75; Child/Student £1.00; Family £6.00.

Facilities: Exhibitions. There is a car park and toilets close to the site.

Disabled Access: Only to ground floor and by prior arrangement.

CASTLE MATRIX

Rathkeale, Co. Limerick Tel: 069 64284
S past Adare on N21 from Limerick: southern edge of Rathkeale

Ownership: Family Trust

General Description: This 90ft Geraldine fortified tower (c. 1420s) was named Castle Matres originally (after the goddess of love and poetry) and may have housed the library of the 4th or Wizard Earl of Desmond at one time. It was confiscated in 1580 by the English and eventually passed to the Southwell family of Suffolk who added the wing c. 1620. Edmund Spenser the poet and Sir Walter Raleigh met here for the first time as young men and potatoes were reputedly first grown in Ireland on this estate. After nearly 300 years the Southwells sold the Castle to the Johnstones or Johnsons of Rathkeale, who abandoned it to avoid penal taxes in the 1920s. As a ruin, it was found and restored by Colonel John Joffre Driscoll of the USAF over the last thirty years of his life. He died in 1991 and left the property and his collection as a Trust to become an educational foundation for the benefit of Ireland and his family, who intend to fulfil his dream. The library has a collection of manuscripts going back to Elizabethan times and includes records of the Wild Geese who fled Ireland to serve in foreign armies.

Open: 1st May to 30th September, Saturday to Thursday, 11.00-5.00; other times and Fridays by appointment.

Admission: £3.00; Senior Citizen £1.50; Student/Child over 12 £1.00.

Facilities: Museum. Research Library. Refreshments available by request - to quote the family 'this is our home but we like to share it with kindred spirits'.

Disabled Access: Ground floor only.

Additional Information: Picnics if people are tidy. Well-behaved dogs on leads.

Special Events: Musical evenings. Workshops.

GLIN CASTLE

Glin, Co. Limerick Tel: 068 34173
N69 from Limerick towards Tralee, 32 miles from Limerick

Ownership: The Knight of Glin

General Description: Despite its toy fortress like appearance, Glin Castle is basically a plain Georgian house. The battlements and crenellations were added in the 19th century, together with the matching Gothic folly lodges.
The Castle seems to float on the River Shannon whilst the wooded banks rise up behind it. The entrance hall boasts a screen of Corinthian pillars with a lovely neo-classical plaster ceiling. The visitor then proceeds along an enfilade of magnificent reception rooms filled with 18th-century Irish mahogany furniture and family portraits. The Staircase Hall has a rare flying staircase which sweeps up the sides of the room and truly seems to fly to the next floor. The dining-room features oak furniture, while across the hall, the drawing-room has another fine ceiling from the Adam period and a beautiful Bossi fireplace.
The formal gardens with their topiary work of bells and balls lead to the daffodil hill, a riot of colour in the spring. Through woods and by streams you come to the walled garden with its fig, pear and plum trees. The rows of the vegetable garden lead to a fine architectural feature which turns out to be the Gothic hen house!

Open: 1st May to 30th June, daily 10.00-12.00 and 2.00-4.00.

Admission: £3.00; Under-18 £1.00.

Facilities: Gateshop craft and tea-shop open 1st April to 30th September.

Disabled Access: No.

Additional Information: Visitors are welcome for dinner, overnight stays and breakfast. Tours with lunch or dinner can be arranged for groups as can lets of the castle.

The Entrance Hall

Glin Castle

CAHIR CASTLE

Castle Street, Cahir, Co. Tipperary Tel: 052 41011
Centre of town

Ownership: Irish State

General Description: One of Ireland's largest and best-preserved castles, Cahir is strategically situated on a rocky island in the River Suir. It is believed to have been built by James Butler, Earl of Ormond. Long thought to be impregnable, it was taken by the Earl of Essex after a ten-day siege in 1599. It was sequestered from the Butlers twice more, but they always recovered it. There is a strong outer wall with massive square and rounded turrets. Inside are two enclosures. In one stands a strong three-storey tower whose rooms include a large hall and fireplace. In the other a hall was turned into a church in 1842.

Open: April to mid-June, mid-September to mid-October, daily, 10.00-6.00; mid-June to mid-September, daily, 9.00-7.30; mid-October to March, daily, 10.00-1.00, 2.00-4.30.

Admission: £2.00; Senior Citizen £1.50; Child/Student £1.00; Family £5.00.

Facilities: Car park close to site. Toilets.

Disabled Access: Limited access by prior arrangement.

Additional Information: The visit includes an audio-visual show (17 mins) informing visitors of all the sites in the area. No dogs.

DAMER HOUSE

Roscrea Heritage Centre, Castle Street, Roscrea, Co. Tipperary
Tel: 0505 21850

Ownership: Irish State

General Description: Damer House is a lovely Queen Anne style building from the early 18th century. However its situation is unusual, it stands in the courtyard of the 13th-century castle with its gate tower, curtain walls and corner towers. Even at the comparatively late period of the early 1800s it was obviously felt to be better safe than sorry. The house has a magnificent carved pine staircase and a scroll pedimented doorway.

Open: September and May, Saturday and Sunday, 10.00-5.00; June to September, daily, 9.30-6.30.

Admission: £2.50; Senior Citizen £1.75; Child/Student £1.00; Family £6.00.

Facilities: There are no actual facilities at the Centre but they are available in town.

Disabled Access: No.

Additional Information: No dogs.

ORMOND CASTLE

Castle Park, Carrick-on-Suir, Co. Tipperary Tel: 051 640787
Situated in town of Carrick-on-Suir

Ownership: Irish State

General Description: In the centre of this 15th-century Butler castle, Black Tom, Earl of Ormond, built a typical and very elegant English Tudor manor around 1550. It is unique in Ireland. It is built of stone and brick, with brick gables and chimneys, good stairs, mullioned windows, plenty of privies and a courtyard. The gallery hall has two superbly detailed fireplaces and some of the finest Tudor plasterwork in the country, with representations of Queen Elizabeth flanked by Justice and Equity. Others include medallions of heraldic motifs. The Earl had hopes of entertaining the Queen which were never realised. She never visited Ireland. Building such an edifice outside a castle's walls was too risky in the troubled 16th century. A royal visit was even more difficult.

Open: Mid-June to September, daily, 9.30-6.30.

Admission: £2.00; Senior Citizen £1.50; Child/Student £1.00; Family £5.00.

Facilities: Car park. Toilets.

Disabled Access: Very restricted.

Additional Information: No dogs.

THE SWISS COTTAGE

Cahir, Co. Tipperary Tel: 052 41144
2km from Cahir, signposted from town

Ownership: Irish State

General Description: A delightful example of an early 19th-century 'cottage orné', this perfect architectural creation by the famous Regency architect, John Nash, is an idyllic country cottage where its owner, Richard Butler, 12th Lord Butler, could stay occasionally and entertain in one of the most romantic settings in the world.

The exterior of the cottage is designed to give the perfect impression of a 'natural' building. Its lines seem to billow up and down. The timbers supporting the verandah and the trellis change form and angle with apparent unpredictability. Inside, however, the building has an air of elegant, light spaciousness. In spite of appearances it is not simple. It incorporates all the most fashionable features of a Regency villa within its picturesque setting and every convenience, including a 'modern' kitchen stowed away discreetly underneath the house. The house has been thoroughly restored to some of its former glory, including the extravagantly picturesque wallpaper in the Dufour Room with its scenes of the Orient. Where necessary reproductions of furniture have been lovingly recreated by modern craftsmen.

Open: Mid-March, October, November, Tuesday to Sunday, 10.00-1.00, 2.00-4.30; April, Tuesday to Sunday, 10.00-1.00, 2.00-5.00.

Admission: £2.00; Senior Citizen £1.50; Child/Student £1.00; Family £5.00.

Facilities: There is a picnic site nearby as well as a car park. Toilets.

Disabled Access: No. Toilet.

Additional Information: Guided tours only. No dogs except guide dogs.

The Swiss Cottage

The Master Bedroom

CAPPOQUIN HOUSE

Cappoquin, Co. Waterford Tel: 058 54004

Ownership: Sir Richard Keane

General Description: Today Cappoquin House is little changed from the handsome building completed in 1779 and designed by Abraham Hargreaves, the Cork architect, even though it was burnt to the ground along with the houses of several other Irish senators in the 1920s. Senator Sir John Keane decided to fully restore the house, which he did using old moulds to restore the Adams period plasterwork. Inside there are many mementoes of the Afghan War of 1839, when General Sir John Keane's expeditionary forces defeated the Afghan Army. They include watercolours of the fall of the fort of Ghuznee.

Outside, the visitor is faced to the west of the courtyard by the old wall of the FitzGerald castle which once stood on the site. Nearby is a long Elizabethan house, which was the home of the agent of Sir

Christopher Hatton who was granted the land when it was confiscated from the Earl of Desmond. The garden to the south is crowned with two huge arboreum rhododendrons and planted with unusual trees and flowering shrubs.
The Keanes are descendants of the O'Cahans of Ulster. Their lands were confiscated after the Battle of the Boyne, but George O'Cahan changed his name and his religion and made a fortune.

Open: April to July, Monday to Saturday, 9.00-2.00.

Admission: £3.50.

Facilities: Car park.

Disabled Access: Yes.

Additional Information: Dogs allowed in garden only. No picnics.

CURRAGHMORE

Curraghmore, Co. Waterford Tel: 051 387102
2 miles from Portlaw village

Ownership: Marquess of Waterford

General Description: The same family has lived on this site since 1170. Curraghmore is a building which has grown, almost organically, and the final effect is a most impressive and dramatic creation. A house was added to the original keep in the 17th century. In the middle of the 18th century, the keep itself was decorated with exquisite stucco, possibly by the Francinis. Stable wings were built out to enclose an impressive three-sided forecourt. The demesne is one of the most beautiful in the country. There is a fine formal garden and a magnificent arboretum. Viewed across the lake the house is a scene of perfect, classical loveliness. The Shell House, built in 1754, was personally decorated by Catherine, Countess of Tyrone.

Open: House: year round by appointment for groups; **Grounds and Shell House:** Easter to mid-October, Thursday and Public Holidays, 2.00-5.00.

Admission: House by arrangement; Grounds and Shell House £2.00.

Facilities: Car park.

Disabled Access: Yes to grounds.

Additional Information: There are no picnic sites. Dogs are allowed in the grounds on a lead.

LISMORE CASTLE

Lismore, Co. Waterford Tel: 058 54424
Entrance on northern edge of Lismore town

Ownership: Duke of Devonshire

General Description: Situated on the Blackwater Valley, commanding a superb position overlooking the river, this is one of the most delightful sites in Ireland.
The Castle has been rebuilt and refurbished several times since its foundation in medieval times. In 1811 the 6th Duke of Devonshire commissioned the design from the architect William Atkinson who was responsible for the building as it appears today. At the same time the interiors were designed by Pugin.
The gardens are delightfully linked by the staircase to the Riding House, built in 1631. There is an ancient yew walk. The lower gardens provide woodland shelter for a fine collection of shrubs.

Open: Gardens only from 26th April to 14th September, daily, 1.45-4.45.

Admission: £2.50; Child (under 16) £1.50.

Facilities: Car park. No picnics. Dogs only on leads.

Disabled Access: No.

Lismore Castle

ULSTER (NORTHERN IRELAND) HISTORIC HOUSES

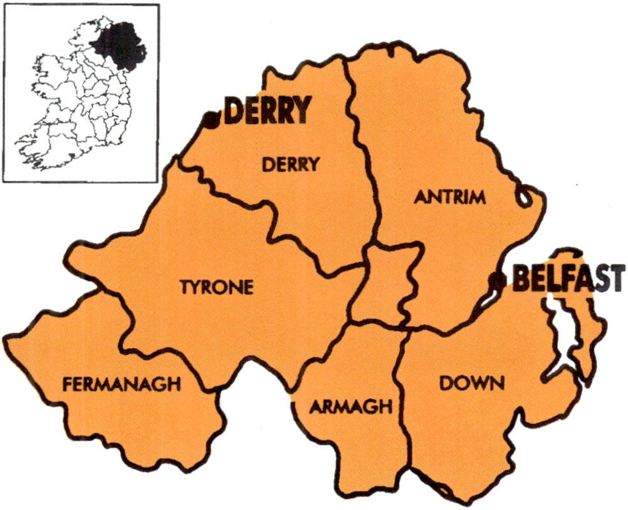

Co. Antrim
Arthur Cottage
Co. Armagh
Ardress
The Argory
Co. Down
Castle Ward
Mount Stewart

Co. Fermanagh
Castle Coole
Florence Court
Co. Derry
Springhill
Co. Tyrone
Mellon Homestead

ARTHUR COTTAGE

Dreen Road, Cullybackey, Co. Antrim Tel: 01266 880781
B62 from Ballymena to Cullybackey. Signposted.

Ownership: Ballymena Borough Council

General Description: The ancestors of Chester Alan Arthur, 21st President of the United States, left this cottage for the New World. Today it has been restored and refurnished so that the visitor can see how the Arthur family lived then. It is a simple, rectangular house of two rooms, each the full length of the building. It has clay floors and an open flax-thatched roof. The main room doubles as kitchen and living-room. Off this is a low chamber with, above, a loft reached by a ladder. Both were bedrooms. The house is furnished with furniture such as the dresser and settle bed, and artefacts which would have been in use at the time. To complete the picture, local women dressed in period costume demonstrate traditional crafts and cooking on selected days.

Open: Easter to September, Monday to Saturday, 10.30-5.00.

Admission: £1.00; Child 50p.

Facilities: Small snack bar. Souvenir shop. Picnic site. Car park.

Disabled Access: Limited.

Additional Information: The Interpretative Centre is housed in a second cottage on the site. It is now a museum of agricultural implements and the history of the Arthur family.

Special Events: Music nights are held once a month.

THE ARGORY

Derrycaw Road, Moy, Dungannon, Co. Armagh BT71 6NA
Tel: 018687 84753
Derrycaw Road, 4 miles from Moy; 3 miles from exit 14 on M1

Ownership: The National Trust

General Description: The Argory is a time capsule with everything in it unchanged since the turn of the century. Electricity was never installed in the main rooms; instead the house is still lit by gas from the acetylene gas plant which was installed in 1906. It gives a warm, yellow light. The house was built in 1824 for Walter McGeough on a slight rise overlooking the River Blackwater on the Armagh/Tyrone border, near Moy.
There is a bewildering array of family treasures left by four generations, including the weighing chair, watercolours by Mary Nicholas, books, portraits and clothing. Undoubtedly, the most celebrated feature is the magnificent cabinet barrel organ built by James Bishop of London in 1824. One of the most important of its kind, it is still in working order.
Beside the house the small Rose Garden is a must, particularly in the summer when the pink and white roses are in full bloom. Beyond, there are 315 acres of woodland and parkland with many interesting walks.

Open: April to June, September, weekends and Bank Holidays, 2.00-6.00; Easter, daily, 2.00-6.00; July and August, daily except Tuesday, 2.00-6.00 (open from 1.00 on Bank Holidays).

Admission: £2.20; Child £1.10; Family £5.50. Estate only: £1.00.

Facilities: Shop and tea-room open as house.

Disabled Access: Partially suitable for disabled visitors. Lavatory.

Additional Information: Picnic sites. Play area for children. Dogs in grounds only on leads.

Special Events: For the full programme of events please telephone

ARDRESS

Annaghmore, Co. Armagh BT62 1SQ Tel: 01762 851236
3 miles from Loughgall intersection No 13 on M11

Ownership: The National Trust

General Description: When George Ensor, a Dublin architect, married Sarah Clarke in 1760 he transformed what had been a modest house into a little mansion, a gentleman farmer's home, with a character and charm all of its own. The interior also boasts splendours. The drawing-room has plasterwork by one of Ireland's most celebrated stuccodores, Michael Stapleton, from 1780. Four exquisite plaques represent the Seasons. There is also some fine furniture, notably the neo-classical gilt settees and torchères, an Irish side table of 1740-50 and a delightful William and Mary chest-on-stand, as well as some fine paintings.
In the cobbled farmyard is an 18th-century piggery, smithy, chicken houses and a well. There are rare farm breeds including bantams, silky hens, sheep and a saddleback sow. Children may feed the hens.
Surrounding the house there are 100 acres of landscaped woodland, garden, orchards and farmland, which were laid out in the early 19th century. The garden has an old-fashioned herbaceous border and a little rose garden.

Open: April to June, September, weekends and Bank Holidays, 2.00-6.00; Easter, daily, 2.00-6.00; July and August, daily except Tuesday, 2.00-6.00. Farmyard: also open May, June, September, weekdays except Tuesday, 12.00-4.00.

Admission: £2.00; Child £1.00; Family £5.00.

Facilities: Woodland playground and picnic site. There is a shop and tea-room at the Argory, three miles away.

Disabled Access: Partially suitable.

Additional Information: Dogs on leads only in park.

Special Events: Halloween Apple Fair.

CASTLE WARD

Castle Ward, Strangford, Downpatrick, Co. Down BT30 7LS
Tel: 01396 881204
7 miles NE of Downpatrick, 1.5 miles W of Strangford village on A25

Ownership: The National Trust

General Description: Castle Ward is certainly an unusual house. Standing on the shores of Strangford Lough, this 18th-century house was the home of the Ward family - both of them. For Bernard and Anne Ward differed in architectural taste and agreed to differ. So the architect did as he was told - the west front is severely classical, the east elaborately Gothic. Inside the visitor can move from style to style. *His* rooms have Doric columns and plasterwork; *hers* display pointed doorways and quatrefoils with exuberant fan vaulting in her boudoir.

An underground passage leads to the stableyard, which contains the Victorian playroom, restaurant and shop and 19th-century laundry. The estate is classical with woods, farmland, landscaped garden and lakes, including Temple Water which is overlooked by a pedimented Temple.

Sadly the Wards finally agreed never to agree, and separated.

Open: House: April, September and October, Saturday and Sunday, 1.00-6.00; Easter, daily, 1.00-6.00; May to August, daily except Thursday, 1.00-6.00. Estate and Grounds: daily all year dawn to dusk.

Admission: £2.60; Child £1.30; Family £6.50; Grounds only £3.50 per car (November to March £1.75 per car).

Facilities: Shop and restaurant open as house. Car park. Picnics welcome. Caravan park.

Disabled Access: Partially accessible.

Additional Information: Working demonstrations at the Cornmill. Old Castle Ward, a defensive tower of 1610, stands nearby.

Special Events: Full range of events including guided walks, concert and opera. Telephone for full details.

MOUNT STEWART

Greyabbey, Newtownards, Co. Down BT22 2AD Tel: 012477 88387
On E shore of Strangford Lough, 5 miles SE of Newtownards, on the Belfast-Portaferry road (A20)

Ownership: The National Trust

General Description: This 18th-century house reflects the major role its owners, the Londonderry family, played in the political and social life of Britain. Foreign Secretary Lord Castlereagh, son of the 1st Marquess, was an influential figure during the Napoleonic Wars and at the subsequent Congress of Vienna in 1815. The original Empire chairs used at the Congress are still displayed in the dining-room. The family's travels are reflected in the bedrooms, which are named after European cities; Rome's bold colours are particularly attractive. The famous portrait of the race horse Hambletonian by George Stubbs dominates the half landing above the stone hall. As an indication of social standing, on a royal visit in 1903 the 6th Marchioness had 274 servants to cater for the royal visitors!
The 98 acre garden is regarded as one of the finest in Ireland. It was largely laid out by Lady Edith, wife of the 7th Marquess, in the 1920s and has an unrivalled collection of rare and unusual plants, colourful parterres and magnificent formal and informal vistas. In late spring the Sunken Garden is a blaze of vivid orange and yellow when the azaleas reach their peak; the scarlet blooms of the Red Hand of Ulster in the Shamrock Garden are equally splendid. In high summer the Italian garden has a magnificent array of roses and herbaceous plants in symmetrical beds. Then there is the Dodo Terrace with its extraordinary concoction of concrete animal statues, the lovely lake and the exquisite Temple of the Winds designed by James Stewart in 1785.

Open: April and October, weekends only, 1.00-6.00; Easter, daily, 1.00-6.00; May to September, daily except Tuesday, 1.00-6.00. **Garden:** April to September, daily, 10.30-6.00; October, weekends only, 10.30-6.00; March, Sunday, 2.00-5.00.

Admission: £3.30; Child £1.65; Family £8.25. Garden only: £2.70; Child £1.35; Family £6.75.

Facilities: Shop and tea-room.

Disabled Access: Yes.

Additional Information: Dogs on leads in park. Picnic sites.

Special Events: There is a full range of events including concerts and guided walks. Please ring for details.

CASTLE COOLE

Enniskillen, Co. Fermanagh BT74 6JY Tel: 01365 322690
On the Newtownbutler-Crom road, 3 miles W of Newtownbutler

Ownership: The National Trust

General Description: Castle Coole is a building of European stature. The family home of the Earls of Belmore was designed by James Wyatt and took ten years to reach completion in 1798. It is a balanced Palladian edifice with colonnades on each side of the main front, leading to elegant pavilions.
The interior of this magnificent neo-classical building was created by some of the leading craftsmen of the late 18th century: chimney-pieces carved by Westmacott, plasterwork by Rose, scagliola columns and pilasters created by Bartoli. With its lavish crimson silk and gold trimmings, the splendour of the State Bedroom, said to have been created for a royal visit in 1821, is one of the highlights of the tour. It has recently been fully restored.
From the Bow Room there are wonderful views out over the surrounding 700 acre estate, a fitting setting for the house with parkland, Lough Coole and extensive woodlands.
Visitors may also see the grand yard, the servants' tunnel or the recently restored ice house.

Open: April, May, September, weekends and Bank Holidays, 1.00-6.00; Easter, daily, 1.00-6.00; June to August, daily except Thursday, 1.00-6.00.

Admission: £2.50; Child £1.25; Family £6.25. Estate: £1.50 per car.

Facilities: Shop and tea-room.

Disabled Access: Yes to ground floor.

Additional Information: Dogs on leads in the grounds only. Picnic areas.

Special Events: For a list of special events please telephone.

FLORENCE COURT

Co. Fermanagh BT92 1DB Tel: 01365 348249
8 miles SW of Enniskillen, via A4 Sligo road and A32 Swanlinbar road

Ownership: The National Trust

General Description: Set dramatically amongst the mountains and forests of west Fermanagh, Florence Court is a fascinating example of mid-18th-century Irish Palladian architecture. The present house, the former home of the Earls of Enniskillen, was started by John Cole and completed around 1775, when the colonnaded arcades and matching pavilions were added. It was named after his wife.
One of the chief glories of Florence Court is the exceptional embellished rococo plasterwork, seen at its best above the stairs and in the dining-room. It probably dates from 1755 and is in the style of Robert West, Dublin's leading 18th-century stuccodore.
The house also displays fine Irish furniture including, in particular, a rococo armchair in the library, an Irish writing cabinet in the study which dates from 1730 and an unusual 18th-century bed.
The estate is a large area of parkland, garden and woodland, including the recently-restored walled garden where the pink and white roses are especially attractive in early summer. The Pleasure Grounds boast several interesting features such as the water-powered saw-mill, an ice house and the summer house. In a much wilder part of the estate grows the oldest yew tree in Ireland, a descendant of two found in the Fermanagh hills in 1740.

Open: April, May, September, weekends and Bank Holidays, 1.00-6.00; Easter, daily, 1.00-6.00; June to August, daily except Tuesday, 1.00-6.00. Estate: all year, 10.00-one hour before dusk.

Admission: £2.50; Child £1.25; Family £6.25. Estate £1.50 per car.

Facilities: Shop and tea-room. Car park. Picnics welcome.

Disabled Access: Partially accessible. Adapted WC.

Additional Information: Mother and baby room. Dogs on leads only in grounds.

Special Events: For a list of events please telephone.

SPRINGHILL

Springhill, Moneymore, Co. Derry BT45 7NQ
Tel: 016487 48210
1 mile from Moneymore on Moneymore-Coagh road (B18)

Ownership: The National Trust

General Description: 'The prettiest house in Ulster.' Springhill, a late 17th-century Plantation House, built and lived in for 300 years by the Lenox-Conyngham family, still feels like a family home, with portraits, furniture, military memorabilia and decorative arts filling its rooms. The gun room's collection includes flintlocks, blunderbusses and a long pike said to have been used at Vinegar Hill in 1798. In contrast, the nursery is a happy jumble of toys, cots, a scaled down piano and a much loved teddy bear. The family gave the house to the Trust in 1957 but a friendly ghost - believed to be that of Olivia, whose husband George Lenox-Conyngham committed suicide in 1816 - stayed. The costume collection, which features clothing from the 18th century to the present, can be found in the old laundry houses.

Open: April to June, and September, Saturday, Sunday and Bank Holidays, 2.00-6.00; Easter, daily, 2.00-6.00; July and August, daily except Thursday, 2.00-6.00.

Admission: £2.20; Child £1.10; Family £5.50.

Facilities: Shop and tea-room in the house. Children's play area with a wild west theme. Waymarked walks through the parkland. Caravan site.

Disabled Access: Partially suitable.

Additional Information: Dogs permitted in grounds only on leads.

Picnics welcome.

Special Events: There is a large number of events from April through to September. Please ring for details.

MELLON HOMESTEAD
The Ulster American Folk Park

Castletown, Omagh, Co. Tyrone Tel: 01662 243292
Between Newtownstewart and Omagh

Ownership: Scotch-Irish Trust of Ulster

General Description: The Mellon Homestead is the original birthplace of Judge Thomas Mellon who in 1818, at the age of five, emigrated with his parents to Pennsylvania. He subsequently founded the fabulously rich Mellon dynasty, building his vast industrial and commercial empire in the United States. His son then built Pittsburgh! The outbuildings are typical of those found on County Tyrone farms in the 19th century.

The Homestead is, however, just one of a great range of other buildings which have been either moved to this site or reconstructed. The whole park describes the lifestyle of the country folk in Ulster and their emigration to the United States. The original parts of the park were based on Mellon's autobiography. There is a replica of the 18th-century thatched Presbyterian Meeting House where he worshipped, the local school, a weaver's cottage and a blacksmith's shop. But it has since been expanded to cover all emigrants. There is the thatched cottage which was the childhood home of Archbishop John Hughes who built St Patrick's Roman Catholic Cathedral in New York. There is also the home of Hugh and Robert Campbell, which illustrates the living conditions of a prosperous Ulster family at the beginning of the 19th century. Besides homes there are replicas and reconstructions of docks, the Post Office, an American log cabin, a boarding house in Derry, a famine cabin and the Tullyvallen Mass House.

Although only the Mellon Homestead is actually on its original site, the whole park gives a fascinatingly vivid picture of life for ordinary people in the 18th and 19th centuries and the realities of emigration to the New World.

Open: Easter to September, Monday to Saturday, 11.00-6.30; Sunday and Bank Holidays, 11.30-7.00; October to Easter, Monday to Friday, 10.30-5.00.

Admission: £3.50; Child/Senior Citizen/Disabled £1.70; Family £10.00.

Facilities: Craft and gift shop. Cafe. Picnic area.

Disabled Access: Suitable.

Additional Information: Costumed interpretative staff. Gallery of exhibitions. No dogs.

Special Events: There is a wide programme of events in the park every year such as an American Wedding, Rare Breeds, Frontier Festival and Appalachian and Bluegrass Music Festival. Please telephone for a comprehensive list.

The Mellon Homestead

Glenveagh Castle

ULSTER (REPUBLIC) HISTORIC HOUSES

Co. Donegal
Glebe House
Glenveagh Castle
Co. Monaghan
Castle Leslie

GLENVEAGH CASTLE

Glenveagh National Park, Church Hill, Letterkenny, Co. Donegal
Tel: 074 37090
25km from Letterkenny

Ownership: Irish State

General Description: In a wild setting, Glenveagh rises in fortified grandeur above the shores of a lonely wooded lough. Its appearance belies its history, for the first stage of this country retreat was actually completed in 1873 and in a style similar to that of Balmoral. Extensions were added towards the end of the century when the building became the centre of fashionable hunting parties. Its last owner, Henry McIlhenny, added the exotically planted gardens. The severe granite exterior of Glenveagh is softened inside, where the predominant colour is crimson. The drawing-room is, for instance, furnished mainly with George III furniture and has a white marble fireplace originally from Ards House. Other rooms reflect this air of comfortable formality in the splendid furniture, objets d'art and paintings collected by Henry McIlhenny.
The gardens are a series of secluded informal terraces and walks with specially imported plants that can survive in this sheltered if wild spot.

Open: 5th April to 2nd November, daily (except Friday in October and November), 10.45-6.00; Sunday in June to August, 10.45-7.00.

Admission: £2.00; Senior Citizen £1.50; Child £1.00 (entrance for park and castle).

Facilities: Tea-room in castle yard open Easter and end May to end September. Visitor Centre. Nature Trail. The National Park itself is vast.

Disabled Access: Yes to park and to ground floor of castle.

Additional Information: Guided tours only (last tour 40 minutes before closing). Picnic sites. Car park with free bus shuttle service to castle.

Special Events: There is a programme of guided walks and garden tours. Please telephone for dates.

Glenveagh Castle

The Master Bedroom, Glenveagh Castle

GLEBE HOUSE

Church Hill, Letterkenny, Co. Donegal Tel: 074 37071
18km from Letterkenny on R251

Ownership: Irish State

General Description: This Regency house, set in woodland and gardens, is decorated with William Morris textiles, Islamic and Japanese art and other treasures. In the gallery is a collection of 300 works by leading 20th-century artists such as Picasso and Kokoschka as well as Irish and Italian artists.

Open: 5th to 13th April, daily, 11.00-6.30; 17th May to 28th September, Saturday to Thursday, 11.00-6.30.

Admission: £2.00; Senior Citizen £1.50; Child/Student £1.00; Family £5.00.

Facilities: Tea-room open during the summer months. Car park. Toilets.

Disabled Access: Access to ground floor of gallery only.

Additional Information: Videos about the house and National Park are also shown.

CASTLE LESLIE

Glaslough, Co. Monaghan Tel: 047 88109
6km N of Monaghan at Glaslough

Ownership: Leslie family

General Description: Although the Leslie family have lived here since the 17th century, the present house was built only in 1878. It was designed by Lanyon and Lynn and was one of the last great houses to be built. Still family-owned, it contains the original furniture, family portraits, books and archives going back to the 1660s. Visitors will see fine stucco work, rich Italian and Spanish furniture, Belgian tapestries and Persian carpets. All the bedrooms retain their original Victorian splendour from when Churchill (a cousin) or Queen Victoria's son came to stay. Other guests included Yeats, George Moore and Gogarty.
The estate of over 1,000 acres includes two lakes, Glaslough overlooked by the Castle, and Kelvey deep in mature woodland.

Open: 30th April to 31st August, Sunday to Thursday, 2.00-6.00.

Admission: £3.00; Child £1.50; Family £7.50.

Facilities: Teas in the Conservatory. Croquet lawn. Car park.

Disabled Access: No.

Additional Information: No dogs allowed. No picnics.

Special Events: The Castle is available for accommodation and conferences. Banquets by arrangement. Please telephone for details.

Castle Leslie

Heather Island

CONNACHT HISTORIC HOUSES

Co. Galway
Athenry Castle
Aughnanure Castle
Dunguaire Castle
The Fields of Athenry
Heather Island
Kylemore Abbey
Nora Barnacle's House
Pearse Cottage
Portumna Castle
Thoor Ballylee

Co. Leitrim
Lough Rynn House
Parkes Castle

Co. Mayo
Westport House

Co. Roscommon
Clonalis
Frybrook House
King House
Strokestown Park

Co. Sligo
Lissadell House

ATHENRY CASTLE

Athenry town, Co. Galway Tel: 091 844797
Located in town

Ownership: Irish State

General Description: Richard de Burgo granted a charter to Meiler de Bermingham in 1235 and, shortly afterwards, de Bermingham started building his castle at Athenry. It was probably completed by 1250 and consists of a three-storey tower surrounded by the remains of a strong outer wall.

Open: Mid-June to mid-September, daily, 9.30-6.30.

Admission: £2.00; Senior Citizen £1.50; Child/Student £1.00; Family £5.00.

Facilities: Car park near site. Toilets.

Disabled Access: Access to ground floor.

Additional Information: Audio-visual show (20 mins) and exhibition.

AUGHNANURE CASTLE

Oughterard, Co. Galway Tel: 091 82214 (or 091 552214)
3.5km from Oughterard on N59

Ownership: Irish State

General Description: Built by the O'Flahertys around 1500, this building is a restored tower house. Most unusually it has a double bawn or courtyard. Although it lies in an idyllic setting near the shores of Lough Corrib, it has seen a turbulent history. Sir Edward Fitton all but destroyed the buildings in 1572, but the O'Flahertys held on and only lost the Castle, finally, towards the end of the 17th century.

Open: Mid-June to mid-September, daily, 9.30-6.30.

Admission: £2.00; Senior Citizen £1.50; Child/Student £1.00; Family £5.00.

Facilities: Car park. Toilets.

Disabled Access: Very limited. Please ring.

Additional Information: Exhibition in Castle.

NORA BARNACLE'S HOUSE

4 Bowling Green, Galway City, Galway Tel: 091 564743
Behind St Nicholas Church off Shop Street

Ownership: Private

General Description: Nora Barnacle, companion and wife of James Joyce for over thirty years, was the inspiration for many of his characters, including Molly Bloom in *Ulysses* and Gretta Conroy in the short story 'The Dead' from *Dubliners*. Her family home in Bowling Green in Galway has been lovingly restored to its turn of the century condition. Built in the 1800s, it is a two-roomed house with a very small back yard. The ground floor room served as a kitchen, dining-room and often bedroom. Originally the cooking was done over an open fire in pot ovens and on large griddles, although now a turn of the century range has been installed. The upstairs room was a communal bedroom. It was probably divided to provide two sleeping areas. Fowl and sometimes pigs were kept in the back yards of terrace houses like this. In summer the yard could also serve as an extended kitchen. Water was obtained from a communal pump across the road.

Open: Mid-May to mid-September, Monday to Saturday, 10.00-5.00 (closed for lunch); ring at other times and it may be possible to visit.

Admission: £1.00.

THE FIELDS OF ATHENRY

North Gate Street, Athenry, Galway Tel: 091 844113
Near Tourist Information Point in town

Ownership: Family owned

General Description: This traditional thatched Irish cottage has been lovingly restored and furnished to evoke the period when such a cottage was a focus for entertainment. Today it is still the focus for traditional entertainments. The kitchen displays the utensils from the turn of the century, and farm machinery can be seen in the yard.

Open: May to September, Monday, Tuesday, Thursday, Friday, 10.30-9.00; Wednesday and Saturday, 10.30-11.45; Sunday, 2.00-6.00.

Admission: Free.

Facilities: Coffee, tea and scones served. Bar facilities. Toilets.

Disabled Access: Please ring.

Additional Information: Traditional music and dancing on Wednesday and Saturday nights.

DUNGUAIRE CASTLE

Kinvara, Co. Galway Tel: 091 37108
17 miles from Galway City

Ownership: Lady Ampthill. Managed by Shannon Heritage.

General Description: Built on the site of the 7th-century stronghold of King Guaire of Connacht, this majestic building, built in 1520, dominates Galway Bay. In 1924 Oliver St John Gogarty, poet, author, wit and friend of W.B. Yeats and Lady Gregory, bought the castle as a quiet refuge.

Open: Daily, mid-April to September, 9.30-5.30.

Admission: £2.35; Child £1.30; Senior Citizen £1.20; Banqueting guest £1.20.

Additional Information: Medieval banquets each night with entertainment based on the songs, poems and extracts from great Irish writers.

Dunguaire Castle

HEATHER ISLAND

Tully Lake, Renvyle, Connemara, Co. Galway Tel: 095 41028
Via Tully village, signposted off N59 in Letterfrack

Ownership: Guy St John Williams

General Description: Oliver St John Gogarty, doctor, poet and wit, held court in true Oscar Wilde fashion in his Dublin home, but his beloved retreat was Renvyle House and Heather Island in Connemara. Beautifully situated in Tully Lake, Heather Island was part of the Blake family estate from 1689 to 1917 when Gogarty bought it with Renvyle House. Renvyle was burnt down during the Civil War, so he extended and renovated a Blake house on Heather Island as a further home in the West - but one where the family would not be burnt in their beds. Now the family home of Guy St John Williams, Gogarty's grandson, it is still a blessed retreat. Balconied throughout its length and overlooking a flagged courtyard, the house is lost amongst hydrangeas and rhododendrons against the backdrop of the Twelve Bens. You can catch a boat over to the house and roam at will across the island with its mixture of wild and cultivated areas and gardens.

Open: Mid-June to mid-September, Tuesday to Saturday, 2.00-6.00.

Admission: £3.00; Child £1.00; Student/Senior Citizen £1.50; Family £7.00.

Disabled Access: No.

Additional Information: No picnics or dogs.

PEARSE COTTAGE

Rosmuc, Co. Galway Tel: 01 6613111
R340 via the N59 and the R336

Ownership: Irish State

General Description: Padraig Pearse (1879-1916), the executed leader of the 1916 uprising, spent as much of his leisure time as possible in this modest thatched cottage, improving his knowledge of the Irish language among the local speakers. The cottage is now a national monument and has been restored with memorabilia of the idealistic schoolteacher and poet.

Open: Mid-June to mid-September, daily, 9.30-1.30, 2.30-6.30.

Admission: £1.00; Senior Citizen 70p; Child/Student 40p; Family £3.00.

Facilities: Car park.

KYLEMORE ABBEY

Kylemore, Connemara, Co. Galway Tel: 095 41146
N59 from Galway - turn right at 'Recess'

Ownership: Benedictine Community - Kylemore Abbey

General Description: With its turrets, towers and battlements rising from the shores of the lake, Kylemore Abbey was built as a fairytale castle in 1868 by a Mr Mitchell Henry, as a gift for his wife, Margaret Vaughan. It is in a flamboyant neo-Gothic style. Today the 'castle' is an abbey, the home of Benedictine nuns. However, visitors can tour part of the house, looking much as it did when the Henrys entertained. The grounds with their spectacular glass-houses are also open and provide a perfect setting for the private chapel, recently restored, which has been called a miniature cathedral, as it is actually based on Norwich Cathedral in England. It is certainly very beautiful.

Open: Easter to Halloween, Monday to Friday (except Good Friday), 9.00-6.00; Halloween to Easter, Monday to Friday, 10.00-5.00.

Admission: £1.50; Student/Senior Citizen £1.00; Family £3.00.

Facilities: Restaurant. Craft shop specialising in Irish crafts (especially pottery), many of which are made in the Abbey. Abbey Exhibition.

Disabled Access: Yes.

Additional Information: Dogs allowed in grounds on leads.

Kylemore Abbey

THOOR BALLYLEE

Gort, Co. Galway Tel: 091 31436
1km off the Galway-Limerick road (N18): 1km off the main Gort-Loughrea road (N66)

Ownership: Ireland West Tourism

General Description: Thoor Ballylee was the summer home of the poet William Butler Yeats for twelve years and the setting of 'The Winding Stair' and 'The Tower' poems. It provided a place of peace and inspiration: 'We are at our Tower and I am writing poetry as I always do here'. But the Tower also has an earlier history. It was originally a Norman fortified house owned by the de Burgo family and then successively by the Persses, Lamberts, Martyns and Gregorys. Raftery, the blind Irish poet, lived nearby and wrote of the local beauty, Mary Hynes. Yeats bought it in 1916 for £35 and lavished time and money on it.
The castle has been restored to look now as it did when Yeats first lived here and a beautiful garden has been created around it. Visitors can see the 'Seven Woods' from the top after climbing the 'Winding Stair'.

Open: Easter to 30th September, daily, 10.00-6.00.

Admission: £3.00; Student/Senior Citizen £2.50; Family £6.00.

Facilities: Tea-room serving light meals and snacks. Audio-visual presentation on the history of Yeats and the Tower. Craft shop.

Disabled Access: To ground floor only.

Additional Information: Picnic site. Dogs allowed on site.

Thoor Ballylee

PORTUMNA CASTLE

Portumna, Co. Galway Tel: 0509 41658
In Portumna town, on Loughrea-Nenagh road (N65) or 24km from Birr along R489

Ownership: Irish State

General Description: The great semi-fortified house at Portumna was built before 1618 by Richard Burke or de Burgo, 4th Earl of Clanricarde. It is a large rectangular country home built also for defence. For instance whilst there is a fine Renaissance-style doorway it has gun-holes to one side of it. There is a fine view overlooking Lough Derg. To the north is a formal, geometrically laid out garden, of the type which is often associated with large Jacobean mansions. There is an exhibition in the Castle and gate house.

Open: Mid-June to mid-September, daily, 9.30-6.30.

Admission: £1.00; Senior Citizen 70p; Child/Student 40p; Family £3.00.

Facilities: Car park close by.

Disabled Access: Limited access to garden and gate house.

LOUGH RYNN HOUSE

Mohill, Co. Leitrim Tel: 078 31427
3.5km from N4 on outskirts of Mohill

Ownership: Private

General Description: The estate is in many ways of more interest than the House, although there is a splendid Baronial Hall which today houses a collection of maps, drawings and documents illustrating the history of the estate. This was built in 1832 by Lord Leitrim, but is just the last in a long line of historical sites in the demesne. There is also a 4,000 year old neolithic burial tomb, and Reynolds Castle, now a ruin, which was built in the 16th century to defend the estate during the Plantation era.
One hundred years ago the 90,000 acre estate of William Sydney Clements, 3rd Earl of Leitrim, spread over four counties and he reigned here for forty years until his assassination in 1878 - an event from which many date the fall of landlordism in Ireland. Today the estate is still in the hands of the Clements family. The rolling acres are no more, but the visitor will find 100 acres of ornamental gardens, a walled garden, woodlands, nature trails and 600 acres of lakes.

Open: End of April to mid-September, daily, 10.00-7.00.

Admission: £1.25; conducted tours £1.00.

Facilities: Restaurant. Craft shop. Picnic site. Playground.

Additional Information: There is excellent coarse fishing throughout the grounds.

PARKES CASTLE

Fivemile Bourne, Co. Leitrim Tel: 071 64149
11km from Sligo town on R286

Ownership: Irish State

General Description: This 17th-century fortified manor house picturesquely set beside Lough Gill, with its combination of strong castle and the walled enclosure, called a bawn, is typical of Plantation settlements. The Manor House itself has three storeys with cut stone mullioned windows and distinctive diamond-shaped chimneys. The large staircase in the entrance hall was a rarity in the 17th century and leads up to the Hall and the bedchambers on the upper floor. The whole building has recently been restored using Irish oak and traditional craftsmanship. The courtyard contains the foundations and features of an earlier defensive system, as well as a forge and a sally port.
The O'Rorke stronghold stood on this site. The Castle was probably built around 1642 by Roger Parkes.

Open: St Patrick's weekend (March 15th-18th) and 5th April to end of May, Tuesday to Sunday, 10.00-5.00; June to September, daily, 9.30-6.30; October, daily, 10.00-5.00.

Admission: £2.00; Senior Citizen £1.50; Child/Student £1.00; Family £5.00.

Facilities: Tea-room. Exhibitions and audio-visual show (20 mins). Car park. Toilets.

Disabled Access: Limited access only. No entry charge. Toilet.

Additional Information: No picnics. No dogs.

Special Events: Parkes Family Exhibition Room.

WESTPORT HOUSE

Westport, Co. Mayo Tel: 098 25430

Ownership: Lord Altamont

General Description: Westport House is one of Ireland's greatest houses. It is built on the site of a castle of the O'Malleys (the dungeons can be visited) and indeed the family are descendants of the famous Grace O'Malley. They included the original John Browne who was a colleague and friend of Patrick Sarsfield, and the 2nd Marquess of Sligo who was a friend of Lord Byron, Joachim Murat, King of Naples and King George IV from whom he declined a dukedom. The present Marquess of Sligo opened the House to the public in 1960, turning it into a thriving business.
In 1730 John Browne commissioned Richard Cassell to build the new Westport House - today's east front and the front hall with its barrel ceiling. Then in 1778 John's son Peter hired the famous architect James Wyatt to complete the House, lay out the park and plan the new town of Westport (still one of the loveliest towns in Ireland). Wyatt's masterpiece in the House is the dining-room. Finally the 3rd Marquess had the wonderful marble staircase built, importing Italian craftsmen specially for the purpose.
But apart from the wonderful building and its interiors the House is full of treasures. The paintings include works by Reynolds and Rubens and a large group by James O'Connor, perhaps the best Irish landscape painter. Waterford glass, old English and Irish silver and mementoes of the 1798 rebellion, sculptures, gorgeous Chinese-style wallpaper as well as some superb 17th and 18th century furniture complete a collection which should not be missed. The original estate and park is laid out around an artificial lake. Today, however, besides the woods and gardens, the visitor will find a

plethora of attractions for adults and children in the grounds. Indeed it is possible to stay on a campsite in the grounds and enjoy the facilities at a more leisurely rate.

Open: 31st May to 28th June, Tuesday to Friday, 2.00-6.00; Saturday to Monday, 2.00-6.00; 29th June to 24th August, Monday to Saturday, 10.30-6.00, Sunday, 2.00-6.00; 25th August to 1st September, daily, 2.00-6.00; 2nd September to 8th September, daily, 2.00-5.00.

Admission: £6.00; Senior Citizen/Student £3.50; Child £3.00; House and Children's Zoo £6.50; Senior Citizen/Student £4.00; Child £3.25. Only first two children charged per family.

Facilities: Old kitchen tea-room. Car park. Art centre. Antique shop. Second-hand bookshop. Campsite.

Additional Information: As the brochure puts it, the estate, developed over thirty years, carries a cornucopia of activities for the tourist and holidaymaker. Besides the zoo, boating, model railway, dungeons, tennis and fishing there is an art centre and antique shop. For children there is, in addition, the hill slide, supabounce, Pinkie Rabbit, pony riding, pitch and putt and a playground. Definitely a place for a day out. Whilst here, have a look at the town of Westport which was designed at the same time as the House and is probably the loveliest small town in Ireland.

The Front Hall

CLONALIS

Castlerea, Co. Roscommon Tel: 0907 20014
Half mile from Castlerea on T39

Ownership: Family owned

General Description: In woods by the bank of the river, here is the ancestral home of the O'Conors, Europe's oldest family. They have lived on this site for 1,500 years. The O'Conors of Connacht are descendants of the last High King of Ireland and traditional kings of Connacht. Their history can be traced back in over 10,000 documents stored in the house. Other exhibits include the last Brehon Law judgement (from about 1580), the harp of the famous composer O'Carolan, costumes, uniforms, silver, china and lace. This 45-room house was built in 1878 to replace an earlier 18th-century house. The ruins of the 13th-century O'Conor castle at Ballintubber are still standing not far away.

Open: May to September, daily, 2.00-6.00; other times by appointment.

Admission: To be announced.

FRYBROOK HOUSE

Boyle, Co. Roscommon Tel: 079 62170

Ownership: Des and Margaret McLoughlin

General Description: Frybrook House is a joy to visit. You will probably be guided round by someone who has seen the restoration work through from dilapidation to its present happy state. The owners continue to improve the house and garden. 1995 was its first year open, so it can only get better.

Frybrook House was built around 1750 for Henry Fry who came to Boyle at the invitation of Lord Kingston. It is an imposing, Georgian-style, three storey house, many of whose rooms have views over the River Boyle which borders the house. The drawing-room contains fine examples of Georgian decorative plasterwork as well as an Adam fireplace. There is an oculus in the centre of the top storey above a Venetian window.

Open: 1st June to 1st September, daily, 2.00-6.00.

Admission: £2.50; Senior Citizen/Student £2.00; Child £1.50; Family £5.00.

Facilities: Car park.

Disabled Access: To ground floor only.

Additional Information: No dogs in house.

KING HOUSE

Boyle, Co. Roscommon Tel: 079 63242
In Boyle town centre (off N4)

Ownership: Roscommon County Council

General Description: Built around 1730 by Sir Henry King, King House has many unusual architectural features. It is in the Palladian style and lies next to the river in the town centre - an unusual location. It is also vaulted on all floors, even the roofs. These vaults are mainly of brick but some are stone. Today the building is U-shaped, but there is evidence that it was meant to be a square.
In 1780 the King family moved out and the House became a barracks. It was eventually rescued in 1987 and, amongst other features, is now home to the Kings of Connacht Exhibition. Children are welcome.

Open: April, October, Saturday, Sunday and Bank Holidays, May to September, daily, 10.00-6.00.

Admission: £3.00; Child £2.00; Student/Senior Citizen/Unwaged £2.50; Family £8.00.

Facilities: Coffee shop. Craft shop. Bureau de change. Art collection. Car park.

Disabled Access: Fully accessible.

Additional Information: No dogs.

Special Events: Boyle Arts Festival July; MacDermot Clan Gathering July; exhibitions.

LISSADELL HOUSE

Lissadell, Co. Sligo Tel: 071 63150
13km N of Sligo off the N15

Ownership: Josslyn Gore-Booth

General Description: The bay windows of Lissadell House look towards Sligo Bay. Yeats recalled them in his poem in memory of the Gore-Booth sisters Eva and Constance, Countess Markievicz:

The light of evening, Lissadell,
Great windows open to the South.

The present house was built by Sir Robert Gore-Booth in the 1830s and is still the family home. It holds the legacy of generations of colourful Gore-Booths, including pictures and artefacts collected by Sir Robert on the Grand Tour. His son Sir Henry sailed to the rescue of Arctic explorer Leigh Smith. In the next generation Sir Josslyn was a keen instigator of cooperatives, Eva was a noted suffragette and Constance took part in the Easter Rising and was the first woman elected to the House of Commons. The house is a fine example of an austere Greek Revival architecture with a genuine atmosphere of faded grandeur. The dramatic two-storey hallway with its columns and double staircase is the core of the building.

Open: 1st June to 14th September, daily except Sunday, 10.30-12.15, 2.00-4.15.

Admission: £2.50; Child £1.00.

Facilities: Car park.

Disabled Access: None.

Additional Information: No dogs allowed.

STROKESTOWN PARK

Strokestown, Co. Roscommon Tel: 078 33013
23km from Longford on the N5 at the east end of Strokestown

Ownership: The Westward Group

General Description: Strokestown Park was built for Thomas Mahon MP (1701-1782) by Richard Castle in the 1740s. It is in the Palladian style favoured by the Irish gentry of the time. However, despite the expansive facade of the house, the main reception rooms are surprisingly intimate. All are open. The 19th-century Library is particularly impressive with its original wallpaper and Chippendale bookcase. There are also many of the staff and children's areas on view, including a fully-equipped nursery and schoolroom. In the galleried kitchen the mistress of the house could look down on the culinary activity without coming into contact with it. It is the last such kitchen left in Ireland. Outside, the elaborately-vaulted stables have been called an equine cathedral.

Throughout the 18th century the Mahons were regarded as model landlords and they built the town of Strokestown itself: the main street leads right up to the gates of the house. In 1800 Maurice Mahon became Baron Hartland of Strokestown and he remodelled the central block to reflect his altered status. In the 1840s Major Denis Mahon decided to settle the famine locally by shipping his starving tenants off to America in appalling conditions. When the last Mahon sold the house its restoration was undertaken by the Westward Group. It has been acknowledged as one of the single best private restorations in the country.

The walled gardens, which had reverted to the wild, were restored in 1995. They include the longest herbaceous border in Ireland, an ornamental pond, a pergola, a rose-garden and a winter border.

Open: 1st May to 30th September, Tuesday to Sunday, 11.00-5.30.

Admission: £3.00; Concessions £2.40; Family £7.00: **House, Museum and Garden** £6.95; Concessions £5.15; Family £15.00; **House and Museum** £5.40; Concessions £4.30; Family £12.80.

Facilities: Restaurant serving full lunches and snack food. Shop.

Disabled Access: To Museum and ground floor of house.

Additional Information: The Famine Museum at Strokestown is in the stable yards. It tells the story of the devastating Potato Famine in the 1840s when two million people either died or emigrated.

Strokestown Park

INDEX OF HOUSES BY COUNTY ORDER

INDEX OF HOUSES BY ALPHABETICAL ORDER

ACKNOWLEDGEMENTS

The author and publishers would like to thank Anne Grady of the Office of Public Works and the National Trust in Northern Ireland as well as all the owners and managers who gave their help so willingly.